# THE EVOLUTION OF T
## COMMONWEALTH

# THE EVOLUTION OF THE MODERN COMMONWEALTH, 1902–80

## Denis Judd
### and
## Peter Slinn

Foreword by
Shridath S. Ramphal
Commonwealth Secretary-General

*First published 1982 by*
THE MACMILLAN PRESS LTD
*London and Basingstoke*
*Companies and representatives*
*throughout the world*

ISBN 0 333 30840 9 (hardcover)
ISBN 0 333 32988 0 (paperback)

*Printed in Hong Kong*

To Arthur Presswell
and in memory of
Roger Fearon

# CONTENTS

# LIST OF MAPS

# FOREWORD

In the 1980s we are living through a time of transition: from the postwar era of status to a new era of contract, from a world organised on the basis of power to one responsive to the dispersal of power, from relationships of dominance and dependency to new realities of interdependence. It is a time of strain and tension in which political, social and economic elements of change entwine and reinforce each other. Among the major challenges of the 1980s are those of reducing the great disparities between the world's peoples by eliminating poverty amidst prosperity and of enlarging the security of all states by working for peace rather than preparing for war.

The Commonwealth, which brings together a quarter of the world's people and a larger fraction of its states, has already shown its determination to assist in achieving solutions to these paramount issues, and revealed the relevance of its special qualities to the task. Among international organisations, it is unique outside the United Nations in embracing countries at all levels of economic development. Born out of the processes of decolonisation that have been so central an element of contemporary history, this voluntary association of now forty-six nations has evolved into a thoroughly contemporary instrument of internationalism, in tune with the modern world and reflective of it.

The Commonwealth has developed its own methods of working together based on informality and consensus, an original international style which has proved capable of bringing freshness and movement to issues immured in ritual and deadlock. The forms of the association range from non-governmental organisations of professional groups or like-minded individuals, through functional co-operation developed by member countries through the Commonwealth Secretariat, to summit meetings of Commonwealth leaders which have decisively influenced such momentous events as the progress of Zimbabwe to independence – and Commonwealth membership.

The true nature of the modern Commonwealth, which is not as widely understood as it should be, is very well revealed by the authors of this study. In thus contributing to a wider awareness of the Commonwealth's contemporary role their work actually facilitates the fulfilment of its potential. While the authors' judgements and perceptions are of course their own, I associate myself closely with their conviction that the Commonwealth can play a growing part in shaping our modern world as it responds to the challenges at hand.

In all this we must not forget that what gives the Commonwealth its basis of shared ideals and its dynamic for constructive change is its shared inheritance. In embracing so large a sample of the world's people, of many races, colours, cultures, religions and political persuasions, in all parts of the globe, it is yet underpinned by shared traditions in education, law and democratic government – and cemented by a common language for doing business between governments and peoples. This combination of unity and diversity, which is rightly recognised as the association's greatest strength, is the result of a long historical process, which must be understood if we are fully to understand the modern Commonwealth. For this reason also I welcome the present study. An awareness of the Commonwealth's historical evolution can greatly strengthen Commonwealth action in working towards a better future for all its people and for the people of all nations.

Denis Judd and Peter Slinn deserve not just our thanks but our commitment to ensuring the worthy 'evolution of the modern Commonwealth'.

SHRIDATH S. RAMPHAL
Commonwealth Secretary-General

# PREFACE

This book has arisen out of the authors' experiences as teachers of Commonwealth history for the University of London and the Polytechnic of North London. We believe that the book will help to fill a gap in the historiography of the modern Commonwealth, and that it will be particularly useful for students of the British Empire and Commonwealth.

We should like to thank Tim Farmiloe of Macmillan for his support and encouragement, our respective academic institutions for the research opportunities they have made available, Catherine Freeman for preparing the index, and the typing services of the Polytechnic of North London, particularly Sybil Everitt, for their promptness and efficiency.

We have dedicated the book to two good friends: to Arthur Presswell, who taught us history at school with inspiration, flair and a passion for accuracy; and to Roger Fearon, who was our companion both at school and at Oxford, and whose premature death deeply saddened us. Our respective wives and children already know how much we owe them.

*London, 1981*

DENIS JUDD
PETER SLINN

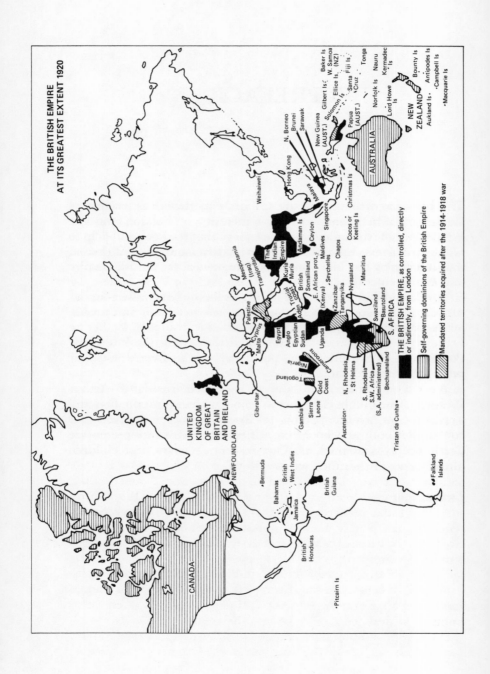

THE BRITISH EMPIRE
AT ITS GREATEST EXTENT 1920

THE BRITISH EMPIRE, as controlled, directly
or indirectly, from London

Self-governing dominions of the British Empire

Mandated territories acquired after the 1914-1918 war

UNITED
KINGDOM
OF GREAT
BRITAIN
AND IRELAND

NEWFOUNDLAND

CANADA

Bermuda

Bahamas
Jamaica · British
West Indies

British
Honduras

British
Guiana

Pitcairn Is ·

· Tristan da Cunha

· Falkland
Islands

Gibraltar

Ascension ·

· St Helena

Gambia

Sierra
Leone

Gold
Coast

Nigeria

Togoland

Cameroons

Palestine
· Cyprus
Malta ·
Egypt
Anglo
Egyptian
Sudan

Mesopotamia
(Iraq)
Transjordan

Aden
Trucial
Coast

British
Somaliland

E. African prot.
(Kenya)

Uganda

Zanzibar

Tanganyika

Nyasaland

· Mauritius

N. Rhodesia

S. Rhodesia
(S.A. administered)

Bechuanaland

S.W. Africa

Swaziland

Basutoland

S. AFRICA

Kuria
Muria

The
Indian
Empire

Maldives

· Seychelles

· Chagos

Andaman Is

Ceylon

Cocos or
Keeling Is

Christmas Is

Weihaiwei

Hong Kong

Macao

Singapore

N. Borneo
Brunei
Sarawak

New Guinea
(AUST.)

Papua
(AUST.)

Solomon Is

Santa
Cruz

Fiji Is

Tonga

AUSTRALIA

NEW
ZEALAND

Norfolk Is

Lord Howe
Is

Baker Is
Gilbert Is

Ellice Is
W. Samoa
(NZ)

Nauru
Kermadec
Is

Bounty Is

Antipodes Is

Aukland Is

· Campbell Is

· Macquarie Is

# INTRODUCTION

This book traces the unique process whereby the largest empire in the history of mankind was transformed into a free association of independent sovereign states. The story involves the study of a number of diverse themes: the decline of Britain as a world power; the shaping of the 'old' British Commonwealth; the nationalist response to colonial rule in Asia, Africa and the West Indies; the birth of a free India; the accelerated process of decolonisation in Africa; the stresses and strains of the modern Commonwealth relationship.

We begin in 1902 with a look at the British Empire at its apogee. We end in 1980 with Britain almost shorn of her dependencies and belonging to a Commonwealth whose Heads of Government, gathered almost a decade before in Singapore (ironically once an imperial fortress), had issued a ringing declaration of Commonwealth principles opposing 'all forms of colonial domination'.

The process of change was, of course, neither steady nor uniform. Territorial expansion, particularly in Africa and the Middle East, continued until after the First World War, by which time Britain's position as a world power was fast being eroded and Indian nationalism was already threatening the fabric of the Raj. In the 1940s, as India proceeded along the uneasy path to freedom, a generation of British colonial administrators in Africa were establishing a pattern of colonial rule designed to outlast the twentieth century. In the 1950s, as new black nations were emerging out of the colonial Gold Coast and Nigeria, Britain was fostering a new 'white dominion' in central Africa. Even after the 1960's wind of change had blown alike over Africa, Asia and the Caribbean, a residue of empire was destined to survive into the 1980s.

During its evolution, the Commonwealth structure has been used and abused for many differing purposes. Originally, a pact of mutual guarantee between Britain and her self-governing dominions; then seen by many in Britain as a device for easing imperial withdrawal symptoms; latterly, Commonwealth meetings have provided a platform for attacks on British policy in relation to Rhodesia, the most painful and protracted of imperial hangovers.

As the association's membership has grown steadily – forty-six at the time of writing – and the political and economic interests of the individual members have diverged, so the tangible links between them appear to have weakened. On many occasions in recent years, when members have been involved in armed conflict with one another, diplomatic relations broken off, or a member, usually Britain, threatened with expulsion, commentators have been poised to pronounce the funeral oration at the final burial of the Commonwealth. Yet the Commonwealth survives, and in 1980 appears to be flourishing.

It is easy to say what the Commonwealth is not – often by reference to what it once was. It is not a military or political alliance, or an economic grouping, a regional pressure group, or a *bloc* of any kind. It has little in the way of formal structure, or rules, or obligations of membership. It cannot therefore be likened to the EEC, NATO, UNO, the OAU, ASEAN, the Group of 77, or OPEC. Yet all these negatives are a key to its positive and unique role as a mechanism for consultation and co-operation between countries which range right across the international spectrum in terms of economic resources, ideological stance and political organisation: only the superpower is missing.

The survival of such an association can surely no longer be explained as a lingering, but doomed relic of a vanished British Empire. Yet the one thing which all members have in common is that they were once painted red on the maps which hung in every British schoolroom. On the one hand, bitter memories of the colonial past have led to a strong reaction in many 'new' Commonwealth countries: the tearing up of 'imposed' Whitehall constitutions, a conscious attempt to revive indigenous language and culture. Even in Australia, one of the founder members of the association, the 1975 constitutional crisis over the dismissal of Prime Minister Whitlam by the Governor-General exposed widespread fears that the monarchical connection somehow deprived the country of full independence. Yet the positive elements in the common experience remain of enduring significance. At Commonwealth gatherings, delegates do, in more than one sense, speak the same language. In such fields as law, education and technical assistance, the interchange of ideas and co-operation is of increasing value in a world which is increasingly divided into mutually suspicious groups of 'haves and have nots'.

The aim of this book is to trace the roots of the modern Commonwealth back into the imperial past. We hope that in doing so we can provide an impartial guide to those who seek to see in historical perspective what is in some aspects still the stuff of very present controversy. The sources, both primary and secondary, available to the historian in this field are vast and ever increasing. Public records in Britain and some other Commonwealth countries are now open after only thirty years and many participants – politicians, administrators and the rest – have left a written record of their experiences. The past twenty years have witnessed an enormous expansion of historical research, particularly in exploring the response of the peoples of Africa and Asia to colonial rule. Much valuable specialised work has been done in such fields as economic and legal history. We hope that this book will make a modest contribution to bringing together the work of 'imperial' historians, whose concern has been the structural and administrative problems of the Empire/Commonwealth, and that of the historians of colonial 'response'. Both approaches would seem to be essential to a full understanding of our theme.

# PART 1

# THE EMPIRE AND IMPERIALISM IN 1902

## BRITAIN AND THE EMPIRE IN 1902

At the beginning of the twentieth century the British Empire covered over a quarter of the world's land surface and contained a quarter of mankind. The British flag flew in every climate and on every continent. The human and material resources of the Empire surpassed those of Ancient Rome or sixteenth-century Spain, just as they dwarfed those of the contemporary French, Dutch or German Empires.

In some respects the Empire was not British at all. Barely 12 per cent of its people were European, let alone British. Its most commonly practised religions were Hinduism and Islam, not Christianity. British administration had hardly penetrated the hinterlands of some of the more recently acquired colonies in Africa or the Pacific.

Yet the British were in the process of stamping a clear, although sometimes light, mark on this vast conglomeration of territories and people. Britain provided the administrative personnel and much of the investment, just as she dominated the Empire's trade. The British monarch, the English language, English legal and constitutional procedures, even English educational standards helped to link the component parts of the Empire together. The full weight of Britain's diplomatic resources could be put at the Empire's service. The Royal Navy, which had helped to create and had grown with the Empire, patrolled the high seas.

The diversity of the Empire, however, was more evident than its unity. This was true not only of its human and geographical characteristics, but also of its acquisition and administration. Broadly speaking, the Empire of 1902 fell into three categories.

Firstly, there were the colonies of white settlement: Canada,

4

Australia, New Zealand, the Cape, Natal and Newfoundland. These were self-governing communities of mostly British stock. In theory their constitutions, based on the Westminster model, made them subordinate to the British government and Parliament. In practice Britain gave them a free hand in their domestic affairs, although dominating their foreign policy for the simple reason that she guaranteed and largely paid for their defence. There were other groups of white settlers, notably in the West Indies and parts of Africa, who did not enjoy self-governing status. In 1902 there were, moreover, the two newly conquered Boer republics (the Orange Free State and the Transvaal) whose future within the Empire was uncertain.

Secondly, there was the great dependency of India. Most of it was ruled directly by Britain, and even in the states governed by Indian princes British advice prevailed. Since 1876 India had been formally an empire in its own right, thus bestowing on the British monarch the somewhat hybrid title of Queen- or King-Emperor. The British Raj in India was fundamentally autocratic, the domination of one race over a subject people. No amount of benevolent and impartial administration could alter that fact. True, Parliament and Cabinet in London could overrule the Viceroy, but distance and the complexities of governing India made this unlikely.

British interest in India, first stimulated by the spice trade in the early seventeenth century, had been handsomely repaid by 1902. Not only was half the British army stationed in India at India's expense, but a numerous and readily available Indian army was also maintained. In addition India provided Britain with her largest and most profitable market within the Empire. Few would have disagreed with the Viceroy Curzon in 1901 when he said, 'As long as we rule India we are the greatest power in the world'.[1]

The colonial empire was the third, and most complicated, category of British possessions. The West Indies, left-overs from the disintegrated North American Empire, were by the beginning of the twentieth century characterised by a long history of impoverishment and unemployment. The once prosperous sugar islands now offered problems rather than profits. In the Mediterranean, Gibraltar, Malta and Cyprus bore witness to strategic needs, while Egypt, the Sudan, Uganda, Kenya and Somaliland on the one flank, and Aden and the Persian Gulf protectorates on the other, further marked out the vital route to India. Ceylon, with its naval base at Trincomalee, was an essential staging post on the run to the Far East and Australia.

Elsewhere British possessions were often without the coherent justification of strategy. The West African colonies were either remnants from the slave trade or the products of commercial and humanitarian enterprise. Central Africa contained Rhodesia and Nyasaland. Rhodesia was ruled by Cecil Rhodes' creation, the British South Africa Company, but was hardly a boon to investors, although more satisfying for white colonists. Nyasaland served no fundamental British interest. In the Far East, Malaya and Borneo were becoming more valuable for their production of tin and rubber than for their strategic positions. Singapore and Hong Kong rested on commerce. In the Pacific there were colonies by no means vital to British security. Indeed, Australian and New Zealand anxieties had been responsible for the acquisition, for example, of South-Eastern New Guinea and the Cook Islands.

In the early 1900s these territories were hardly more divergent than the methods by which they were governed. Chartered companies adminstered Rhodesia and North Borneo. Crown colony government predominated in the West Indies. Ceylon, too, was a crown colony. Protectorates abounded: East Africa, Somaliland, Northern and Southern Nigeria, Nyasaland, Bechuanaland, Aden. Then there were the protected states, such as Brunei, Zanzibar, the Malay states and Tonga, where local rulers remained, but were subject to the advice of British Residents. Egypt also was a state effectively under British control, and the one most vital to British imperial strategy. Yet another form of government was found in the Sudan and the New Hebrides, which Britain ruled jointly with Egypt and France respectively. But the Anglo-Egyptian condominium of the Sudan was a transparent device, and the Sudan was effectively a British dependency.

Regardless of the prevailing influence of Britain in all these territories, their methods of government from London presented little consistency. The Colonial Office ruled the crown colonies, but the Foreign Office was generally responsible for the protectorates and the condominia. The administration of the chartered territories was only loosely supervised by the British government, although a charter could be revoked. Clearly the imposition of a greater degree of uniformity throughout the colonial empire was an urgent task for Britain.

Beyond the Empire there were areas which Britain either

protected informally or dominated commercially. The derelict Turkish Empire had been shored-up against Russia in the Crimean War, and again protected in 1878 during the Eastern crisis. British influence extended to southern Persia and the Persian Gulf. By the beginning of the twentieth century the commerce of China owed much to British management, but only after successive Chinese governments had been overawed by British gunboats and subjected to British commercial pressures. In concert with other interested European powers, and relying heavily on Indian mercenaries, Britain had crushed the anti-foreigner Boxer rising of 1900. Over much of South America, particularly Argentina and Chile, British investment was heavy and her exports profitable.

The extent of Britain's imperial and extra-imperial interests was, therefore, enormous and its implications profound. One such implication was the need to maintain the supremacy of the Royal Navy against all possible challengers. To this end the number of warships was kept at the 'two-power standard', that is, more than the combined strengths of the next two largest navies. But although apparently safe from external aggression the Empire found itself diplomatically in 'splendid isolation'. In fact the isolation was sometimes disturbing and not always splendid. Towards the end of the nineteenth century, Germany's potential naval challenge and the continuing revolution in naval armaments rendered the fleet's supremacy paper thin. A search was made for allies and in 1898 Joseph Chamberlain, the dynamic Colonial Secretary and an avowed imperialist, ardently though unsuccessfully wooed Germany. Despite such initiatives, the twentieth century opened with Britain still bereft of allies and indeed the target of much abuse for her part in the Boer War.

There were other causes for concern. Britain was ceasing to be the 'workshop of the World'. In the 1870s the early Victorian boom had begun to fade. Germany and the United States developed new industries which were often aided by intensive scientific research. Even in her traditional staple industries (coal, cotton and steel) Britain came under pressure. Foreign exporters outstripped their British rivals. By the start of the twentieth century Britain was like a runner who had been given a five-lap start in the industrial race – still ahead, but only by one lap.

One remedy lay in increased foreign investment. But perhaps a healthier salvation could be found in exploiting to the full the vast untapped resources and the huge potential markets of the Empire.

Some believed so and began to call for an end to free trade and the establishment of protective tariffs. Joseph Chamberlain emerged as the chief spokesman for imperial preference (often called tariff reform), whereby inter-imperial trade would pay less duty than that of the foreigner. But tariff reform threatened the traditional free trade policy of both the Liberal and Conservative parties. In any case, Britain's trade with the Empire was less than one-third of her total. Was the Empire able, or indeed willing, to play the part envisaged for it?

Hopes were also raised that a federated Empire would enable Britain to command as powerful a role in the twentieth century as she had in the nineteenth. But by 1902 imperial federation seemed increasingly unlikely. The self-governing colonies, although they had rallied to Britain's cause during the Boer War of 1899–1902, had no desire to submerge their growing national identity in federal schemes. Indian nationalists were beginning to make more radical demands. Other non-European subjects of the crown might one day follow suit.

## IMPERIALISTS AND OTHERS

In 1902 it was difficult to doubt the permanence of the Empire, even if it was equally difficult to be sure of its future evolution. 'Imperialism' was a respectable term, having little in common with the barbarities of imperial Russia or the slovenliness of the Ottomans. The domination of Englishmen over Asians and Africans seemed a natural part of the world order. Indeed it could be argued that without British tutelage and protection the African would never emerge from his primitive state and the Asian would remain subject to obscurantist autocracy.

It was but a small step from such reassuring sentiments to the advocacy of long-term white supremacy and, in particular, the global hegemony of the Anglo-Saxon race. The prophets of the English-speaking people were unashamed and vocal. Academic propagandists like Seeley and Froude had found a ready response among the governing classes. On a more practical level, Joseph Chamberlain (Colonial Secretary from 1895–1903) threw his dynamism and his powerful office behind imperial consolidation and expansion.[2] Imperialism abroad and social reform at home were Chamberlain's battle cries. Indeed he argued that the one was impossible without the other; profits from imperial trade would pay for domestic welfare schemes and material improvement. It was an attractive, though illusory, slogan.

But who were the men to put such notions to the test? Cecil Rhodes was one who had already done so before his death in 1902; pushing the frontiers in southern Africa northwards, bringing huge territories under the Union Jack, dreaming of a Cape-to-Cairo railway and of the map of Africa smothered with red. But Rhodes was unique, not least in his readiness to pour his industrial wealth into imperial adventures. His vision, however, was in some respects crudely limited, his free-spending policy intrinsically mean.[3]

Less primordial, more ordered, were the proconsuls, the administrators of Empire. In 1902 three proconsuls of archetypal stature were at work. In India, the Viceroy, Lord Curzon; in South Africa, Sir Alfred Milner, Governor of the Cape and High Commissioner; in northern Nigeria, Frederick Lugard. In their different ways these three men embodied some of the most cherished ideals of Empire; ideals of incorruptible government, high purpose, constructive statesmanship and the reasonable pursuit of British interests.

In other ways, however, their attitudes were questionable, even flawed. Curzon's reforming and indiscriminating administration was firmly based on a clear assumption of personal superiority and upon the hypothesis that Indians, being quite incapable of self-government, should be ruled efficiently by their betters. Nor was Curzon always ready to heed the Cabinet in London. In fact, convinced that his own policies were right, he sought on several occasions to outwit and even delude his colleagues at home. Such high-handedness merely confirmed residual fears that throughout the Empire 'the man on the spot' had inordinate powers and little regard for the democratic processes.[4]

Alfred Milner, a first-rate administrator and a confirmed race-patriot, had on occasion a similar desire to act free from restraint from Whitehall and Westminster. Anxious to consolidate British supremacy in subjugated South Africa he chafed at the Unionist governments' refusal to let him forcibly federate the four colonies (The Cape, Natal, The Transvaal and the Orange River Colony) by suspending the self-governing constitution of the Cape and ignoring legitimate objections. Milner despised the 'rabble' in the British House of Commons and would have done without them.[5]

Lugard, in 1902, was in the process of mastering the Fulani emirates of northern Nigeria. This was to be a prelude to the extension of British supremacy over all Nigeria and to the introduction of 'indirect rule'. Lugard was to become irrevocably associated with the system of indirect rule in British Africa and, in this respect, a legend in his own lifetime. In December 1902, however, his proposal to send a military expedition to the northern Nigerian city of Kano caused the Prime Minister Balfour to complain: 'I think we have been rather ill-used in the matter of information by Lugard, and I am very sorry to think that we seem likely to have another little war on our hands. But it can't be helped.'[6] Here again, Cabinet policy and proconsular ambitions were not necessarily in accord.

Backing up the administrators were the armed services. Among the foremost builders of empire must be numbered those general officers whose enterprise and determination had forced through a variety of annexations and quelled innumerable revolts and disturbances. Three such men dominated the military pantheon in 1902. The first was Garnet Wolseley, Commander-in-Chief of the British army, an Anglo-Irishman with forty-five years of imperial campaigning behind him. His campaigns included the Burma War of 1852, the Indian Mutiny, the brilliantly successful Ashanti War of 1873 and the equally triumphant 1882 Egyptian invasion, as well as the failure to relieve Gordon at Khartoum in 1884. Wolseley had the reputation of a military reformer and had provided W. S. Gilbert with his 'model of a modern Major-General'.

Field-Marshal Lord Roberts of Kandahar ranked with Wolseley in public esteem, although higher in the affections of the common soldier. Another Anglo-Irishman, Roberts had made his reputation in the Empire's wars and particularly in the epic march from Kabul to Kandahar during the second Afghan War. Diminutive, teetotal, considerate, gentle-natured and usually victorious, Roberts had, by 1902, returned from his successful intervention in the Boer War to become the last Commander-in-Chief of the British army before the abolition of that post in 1904. Instead of campaigning against Pathan and Abyssinian, Roberts now devoted his energies to the cause of universal conscription, or 'National Service'.[7]

Yet another Anglo-Irishman completed Britain's military triumvirate. This was Kitchener of Khartoum.[8] Enigmatic, implacable, icy even in the deserts of the Sudan or under India's blazing sun, Kitchener was detached, a law unto himself, inscrutable. Caring little for popularity or public regard, Kitchener was overwhelmed by both. His reconquest of the Sudan between 1896–9 had established him as a public idol. His ruthless harrying of the Boers had enhanced this reputation even if it had confirmed others in their dislike for his methods. Kitchener was the arch-imperialist; devoted and incorruptible, but also ponderous and a trifle dull.

The ebullience and self-confidence of the other great service, the Royal Navy, was most accurately typified by Rear-Admiral Jackie Fisher. Bustling, charming and clear-sighted, Fisher demanded radical and long-term planning for his beloved navy. In 1902 he was advocating the construction of a big-gun battleship to surpass all rivals – the Dreadnought. Fisher was quite sure that he had got his priorities right, and was fond of insisting that 'The British Empire floats on the British Navy'.[9]

Behind these leaders were the other ranks. The navy had close on 100,000 sailors and over 330 ships of the line. Its activities ranged quite literally over all the world's oceans and seas. The army (including the Indian army) numbered less than 500,000. It was small for its responsibilities and, fortunately perhaps, free of a European war since the Crimea. The army served for the most part overseas where its volunteer soldiers had fought (sharp-eyed and none too gently) through a score of imperial skirmishes. A fair proportion of the army was Irish:

> My name is O'Kelly, I've heard the Revelly
> From Birr to Bareilly, from Leeds to Lahore,
> Hong Kong and Peshawur,
> Lucknow and Etawah,
> And fifty-five more all endin' in 'pore.[10]

Kipling was, of course, the best known poet of Empire and perhaps deservedly so. But there were other versifiers and writers who glorified British achievements: Alfred Austin, Newbolt, even Tennyson, not to speak of the journalists of the cheap, mass circulation *Daily Mail*. W. A. Henty's books for boys leant heavily on imperial themes, and a standard and acceptable hero was the blue-eyed, clean-living young Englishman standing defiantly before his dusky assailants. Not all of this writing, however, was brash and uncritical. Kipling was not without keen insight and his vision was frequently circumscribed by the practical. In his famous

'Recessional', written in 1897 for Victoria's Diamond Jubilee, he had struck a cautionary note:

> If, drunk with sight of power, we loose
>   Wild tongues that have not Thee in awe,
> Such boastings as the Gentiles use,
>   Or lesser breeds without the Law –
> Lord God of Hosts be with us yet,
> Lest we forget – lest we forget![11]

Even within the Unionist alliance, the Conservative party contained men who frowned on imperial expansion and preferred to measure the nation's achievements in terms of trading profit rather than flag-wagging. Little Englanders were still to be found in both the great political parties, and many Englishmen would not have exchanged their grim industrial environments for the open aspect of the prairies. Investors, too, might well have preferred Argentinian railways to Ugandan rubber; the Empire was, indeed, sometimes in the red.

It was difficult in 1902, however, to doubt the permanence of the Empire. Even the numerous critics of imperialism such as left-wing Liberals, Irish Nationalists or trade unionists did not expect, or necessarily desire, the dissolution of the Empire. The militarism and the cruder excesses of imperial expansion certainly aroused distaste and sometimes, as in the case of the incompetently fought Boer War, a sense of national shame. This was a different thing, however, from a call to abandon a system which seemed to guarantee Britain's world position and which, incidentally, helped to disguise her economic deficiencies.

But critics there most definitely were.[12] These ranged in class, ability, and method from the fastidious Gladstonian intellectual John Morley to the rabble-rousing revolutionary socialist preaching at street corners. 1902 also saw the publication of J. A. Hobson's famous *Imperialism*, a compelling critique of contemporary attitudes. Hobson disliked what he described as the untoward influence of imperialist groups in society, education, the press. He also questioned the moral basis of the imperial system; trusteeship was an honourable concept, but did not trusteeship (like power) corrupt?[13]

There were plenty of examples of British heavy-handedness to support such critics. After the fall of Khartoum in 1898 the Mahdi's tomb had been desecrated and his skull destined, at one stage, to become Kitchener's ink stand. During the Boer War nearly 20,000 Afrikaners, mostly women and children, had died in the concentration camps. The pro-Boers, men like Lloyd George, Morley, Harcourt and John Burns, had made much of these disreputable episodes, and even the leader of the Opposition, Campbell-Bannerman, was moved to denounce 'methods of barbarism'. There seemed some substance to the jibe that the sun never set on the British Empire because the Almighty could not trust its rulers in the dark!

The Liberal critics of empire were, however, balanced, perhaps outweighed, by the Liberal-Imperialists. These men, though retaining the right to question imperial methods, broadly supported the system. In 1902 they were an impressive body, containing Asquith, Grey, Haldane, Fowler and Rosebery. The party as a whole had, moreover, underwritten the Jameson Raid of 1895–6, if only by the failure of its representative on the Committee of Inquiry to insist on a full-blooded investigation. Even the leading pro-Boers had ambivalent imperial attitudes. At the heart of Lloyd George's indignation was, perhaps, a Welshman's dislike of English oppression. John Burns could hardly be called a progressive. John Morley, as Secretary of State for India from 1905–10, by no means dismantled the Raj. Few trade unionists if given the choice between benevolence to black men and higher wages would have denied themselves the latter.

Perhaps the truth was that neither arch-imperialists nor dedicated anti-imperialists were typical of their countrymen. Except at moments of great crisis or high military adventure, the British people seem to have taken their Empire for granted; as a sort of comforting though rather complicated backcloth to their everyday activities. Debates on the Indian budget could empty the House of Commons, and there was little in the achievements of an administrator in Ashanti to inspire the dockers of Canning Town or the Glaswegian unemployed.

Nonetheless, the Empire existed. It seemed to offer in 1902 both enormous advantages and immense problems. Equally it exercised both liberal consciences and patriotic complacency. Above all it needed rationalisation and ordered development. The next fifty years, however, were to present the Empire with trials and pressures unprecedented in its previous history.

# PART 2

# CONSOLIDATION AND CATACLYSM, 1902–19

## BRITAIN AND THE DOMINIONS, 1902–14

This period saw the self-governing colonies advance briskly towards a greater sense of national identity and towards an internationally recognised sovereignty. Although in retrospect this process seems orderly and irresistible, in practice the outcome was not achieved without some effort. Doubtless the federations within two of the great Dominions (the Commonwealth of Australia in 1901 and the Union of South Africa in 1910) strengthened claims to full statehood, but such aspirations had to be reconciled with Britain's role as the Empire's defender and foreign policy-maker.

In some ways, the years 1902–19 witnessed a final fling by the advocates of imperial federation and closer co-operation. At the Colonial Conferences of 1902, 1907 and 1911 various such schemes were discussed, though very few were adopted. Efforts to centralise imperial defence, trade and organisation frequently met with hostile or evasive reactions from the colonial delegates. The Conferences were mainly content to declare good intentions but do little about them. True, at the 1907 Conference a Dominions Department of the•Colonial Office was accepted, but only as an alternative to the possibly more exacting Permanent Commission proposed in 1905 by Alfred Lyttelton, then Colonial Secretary.[1] In 1911, a muddled scheme for an imperial council (or parliament) of defence, put forward by Sir Joseph Ward of New Zealand, was torn to pieces by the British Prime Minister Asquith and by Laurier of Canada and Botha of South Africa. Plainly, devolution was preferable to centralisation.[2].

It is important to examine the three main areas of proposed co-operation, to discuss the problems involved in each, and to discover the degree of progress achieved by 1914.

## *Imperial Defence*

The defence of the Empire was in some ways the most urgent subject for imperial statesmen. Perhaps because of this it was also the area in which most advance had been made by the outbreak of the Great War. Basically, imperial defence was Britain's responsibility. Only she, in 1902, possessed the wealth and the weapons for such a gigantic task. There were, however, ways in which the Dominions could ease the burden. One was by contributing to the upkeep of the Royal Navy which was the chief guarantor of the Empire's security. The other was by undertaking clear responsibilities for aiding or supplementing the British army.

By 1902 Australia, New Zealand, the Cape and Natal all made annual financial contributions to the Navy. Encouraging though this was for imperialists and tax payers alike, the payments were not simply expressions of an exuberant imperial patriotism or of a selfless generosity. The Australasian colonies had entered into a Naval Agreement with Britain as early as 1887, but in return for their money they could count upon the presence of a naval squadron in their territorial waters. The two South African colonies had begun their subsidies in the shadow of the deepening crisis before the Boer War; the gesture had been timely.

More remarkable than these contributions was Canada's refusal to pay a penny towards the Royal Navy. This attitude was, in its way, as practical as the opposite policy adopted by the other self-governing colonies. Canada stood in no peril from foreign aggressors. Indeed her great neighbour the United States was theoretically as reliable a protector as was Britain. (When this was not true, as in the Alaska border dispute of 1903 between Canada and the United States, Britain, instead of supporting her daughter state, sold out to Washington with alacrity.)[3] It was, therefore, not surprising that Canadian statesmen calculated that, whether or not a subsidy was forthcoming, Britain would not, in a world crisis, abandon the Dominion that supplied her with essential food and raw materials across the north Atlantic.

One natural, though controversial, development before 1914 was the movement in Canada and Australasia for indigenous navies. In 1909 Australia and New Zealand began to build naval squadrons, the latter destined to be in effect part of the Royal Navy, the former to have somewhat more independence. In Canada two bitterly contested Naval Bills were put before Parliament in 1909 and 1912;

both were mauled, and the second one thrown out by the Senate. By 1914, however, Canada, like Australia and New Zealand, did possess a handful of warships all of which were put at the disposal of the British Admiralty on the outbreak of hostilities.

Less happy was the attempt to co-ordinate the land forces of the Empire. Although the self-governing colonies had rallied to Britain during the Boer War and sent close on 70,000 volunteers to South Africa, they were not anxious to commit themselves to support Britain automatically in any possible belligerent action. One reason for this was that British and Dominion interests were increasingly divergent. Another reason can be found in the character of self-governing colony status which implied the provision of local armies for domestic defence; there was, however, no obligation to put these forces at Britain's disposal.

Any British proposals for improving inter-imperial defence co-operation would, therefore, need to be tactful. By 1904 a substantial improvement was at last achieved. This was the establishment of the Committee of Imperial Defence. Although in 1902 three bodies had existed to serve the needs of imperial defence (the Defence Committee of the Cabinet, the Colonial Defence Committee and the Joint Naval and Military Committee) none of them possessed the necessary degree of authority. The disasters of the Boer War, however, combined with the accession to the premiership in 1902 of Arthur James Balfour provided the impetus for reform.[4]

Balfour had long advocated the establishment of a really effective Defence Committee, but had been thwarted chiefly by the unenthusiastic response of his uncle Lord Salisbury (Prime Minister 1886–92 and 1895–1902). On becoming premier in 1902 Balfour accordingly reconstituted the Cabinet Defence Committee which by 1904 had evolved into the Committee of Imperial Defence. The CID was purely an advisory body, but potentially extremely influential because chaired by the Prime Minister and containing the Cabinet Service ministers as well as powerful representatives of the army and navy.[5] It even had a Permanent Secretariat for keeping minutes – an overdue and, for the times, radical measure. Above all, the CID could hope to induce voluntary colonial participation in its deliberations, and might even produce greater co-operation between those traditional rivals, the army and the Royal Navy.[16]

By 1914 less had been achieved on these counts than might optimistically have been expected. Dominion statesmen still tended to fight shy of the CID and its possibly embarrassing commitments. The CID itself, though meeting regularly even under the post-1905 Liberal governments, lacked bite and the constitutional ability to *impose* its recommendations. The army and the navy continued to eye each other warily.

On the other hand, the precedent of the CID existed and its machinery was being used. In 1909, in the wake of the German navy scare of that year, an Imperial Defence Conference met within the framework of the CID. The delegates, who included representatives of India, declared themselves willing to follow in their military peacetime preparations the advice of the Imperial General Staff (a co-ordinating body set up in 1907 by the Liberal War Minister Haldane). Both the 1911 and the 1917 Imperial Conferences used the CID as the chief forum for defence discussions.

In other ways the defences of the Empire had been considerably strengthened by 1914. Not only had the navy kept abreast of rival building programmes, but a series of diplomatic arrangements had been entered upon. The 1902 Anglo-Japanese alliance had been renewed and extended in 1905, and the Anglo-French entente of 1904 and the 1907 entente with Russia were healthy safeguards. With Washington benign if not rapturous, there was only one real enemy to be reckoned with and British defence planning recognised the fact. After 1907 the 'hostile foreign power' against which provision must be made was not France or Russia but Imperial Germany.

### The Empire's Trade

By 1902 Joseph Chamberlain had come to believe that the most practical bonds for drawing the self-governing colonies closer to Britain were those of commercial self-interest. Despairing of appeals to the heart, Chamberlain now turned his attention to the pocket. No doubt he was encouraged by the evident Canadian interest in reciprocal tariff agreements. This interest, expressed in those tariff concessions between 1897 and 1900 which gave Britain a $33\frac{1}{2}$ per cent advantage over the foreigner, was reiterated by the Canadian delegates at the 1902 Colonial Conference. Since Canada was in some ways the least enthusiastic of the imperial daughters these moves augured well.

In other ways, however, the omens were unpromising. Since the 1840s Britain had been a free trade nation, and a prosperous one.

Both the Liberals and the Unionists had strong free trade traditions. The electorate, rightly or wrongly, associated protection with privation. The self-governing colonies furthermore had taken pains to protect their infant industries behind tariff barriers. These barricades would only be levelled at a price – reciprocal concessions by the Mother Country. But Canada's original gesture had brought no response from Britain. Clearly any advocacy of tariff reform or imperial preference would have to overcome entrenched opposition in the forms of self-interest and prejudice.

1902, however, seemed an auspicious time for such an initiative. Although the value of Britain's exports had once again begun to rise, the previous thirty years had been more uncertain. Of the great powers Britain alone clung to her free trade principles while protectionist nations like Germany and the United States undercut certain British products even in Birmingham and Bradford. Moreover, if sufficient revenue could be raised by tariff reform, necessary items of social reform (such as old age pensions) could be paid for without resorting to increased income tax – a prospect as attractive to most Liberals as to Unionists.

The budget of 1902, furthermore, contained an announcement to revive the import duty on corn, meal and flour.[7] Although this measure was seen by the majority of the Cabinet merely as a means of raising extra revenue to pay for the costly Boer War, Chamberlain hoped that it opened the way to tariff reform. The corn tax could be rescinded for the self-governing colonies, and Canadian wheat, for example, would thus be given preferential treatment over Russian grain. In Ottowa, Prime Minister Wilfrid Laurier expressed this very hope, and before he left for his South African trip in October 1902 Chamberlain had apparently secured Cabinet sanction for such a remission.[8]

On his return in March 1903, however, Chamberlain found his plans in ruins. The orthodox free trade Chancellor of the Exchequer, C. T. Ritchie, had sabotaged the corn tax remission by threatening resignation a fortnight before the 1903 budget. Feeling ill-used by his colleagues, and convinced that only radical fiscal policies would assure Britain of her rightful place in the challenging twentieth century, Chamberlain now decided to campaign openly for tariff reform. By September 1903 his speeches and statements had thrown the Unionists into confusion and split the Cabinet. Balfour, anxious to preserve his authority and his government, engineered the resignations of three of his most awkward free trade

Cabinet ministers while also accepting Chamberlain's resignation.[9]

There is no doubt that Balfour employed some political sleight of hand in these manoeuvres, and was equally glad to be rid of Chamberlain and the latter's bitterest Cabinet opponents. But the Prime Minister subsequently tried to keep his connections with Chamberlain intact. After all, dynamic Joe's campaign *might* convert the country before the next general election. Accordingly Balfour promoted Chamberlain's son Austen to the vacant Chancellorship and professed himself in broad agreement with the ex-Colonial Secretary's campaign. For himself, Balfour contented himself with beautifully phrased but intrinsically meaningless pronouncements on the issue of tariff reform.[10]

An easy life, however, was not to be had. Unionist tariff reformers and free traders pulled further away from each other. One young Unionist MP, Winston Churchill, even joined the Liberals in protest in 1904. The Liberal party watched this fratricidal strife in a mood of anticipatory delight. Chamberlain's well-organised and richly financed Tariff Reform League threatened, at one stage, to devour its parent the Unionist party. Balfour hung on until December 1905, when his government resigned.

The general election of January 1906 was a holocaust for the Unionist party. The Liberals, with the support of Labour and Irish Nationalist members, commanded a majority of 356 in the new House of Commons. Of the 157 Unionist MPs remaining, over two-thirds were Chamberlainites. Since Balfour had lost his seat, the leadership of this Unionist rump seemed to belong to Chamberlain. Balfour averted this threat by a doctrinal compromise of February 1906 in which he made a verbal concession to tariff reform while being confirmed as leader of the party. His position was further strengthened by the serious stroke suffered by Joseph Chamberlain in July 1906; although he lingered on until 1914, Chamberlain's political activities were now confined to exhortations from his sick bed.

The grand project of tariff reform received both setbacks and encouragement up to 1919. On the negative side, the years between 1906 and the Great War saw a Liberal government and hence strict adherence to free trade principles. Some Dominions, tired of waiting for tariff concessions, turned instead to other commercial arrangements, of which the 1911 reciprocity agreement between Canada and the United States was the most galling for tariff reformers. The confusion surrounding the British constitutional crisis of 1909–11, moreover, somehow enabled Lloyd George and others to equate freedom with free trade and tariff reform with tyranny.[11]

On the other hand, the Unionists, in opposition, became unequivocally the party of tariff reform. The most dramatic evidence of this was the ditching of the prevaricating Balfour as leader in 1911, and his replacement by the protectionist, if rather dull, Andrew Bonar Law. The Tariff Reform League's propagandist activities continued unabated and perhaps convinced some working men that there was a substantial degree of accuracy in the slogan 'Tariff Reform means work for all!' The Great War, too, saw inroads made on the dogmas of free trade, with protective duties placed on certain luxury goods in 1915. The post-war era was to witness a further revolution.

### Imperial Organisation

By 1914 hopes for imperial federation had foundered. Such plans basically implied a reversal of the evolutionary processes of Empire as manifested in the development of the self-governing colonies. The initiative for federation consequently came almost exclusively from Britain, although Dominion statesmen did from time to time propose such schemes. It was Britain, however, who stood to gain most from federation, and from the greater imperial cohesion that would result.

Federal schemes, although often attractive in prospect, were less appealing in practice. To begin with, some surrender of autonomy was unavoidable. There had also to be adequate financing. The British Empire, moreover, was not a territorial unit like the Russian or Austrian empires. Even the sending of representatives to a Federal Parliament would have proved expensive. In any case, how was such a Parliament to be composed? If representation was allotted on the basis of population, the Dominions, even collectively, could be consistently out-voted by the massive British delegation. Such problems ensured that the Dominions fought shy of federation.

Perhaps, then, the British Empire was best characterised by a lack of formal organisation? This was at least in keeping with well-founded traditions of empiricism and pragmaticism. British and colonial statesmen eschewed precise theory. The art of 'muddling through' was preferable to any exacting philosophy.

Such organisation as existed was unrestrictive. Co-operation in handcuffs was not agreeable. The periodic Imperial Conference proved an acceptable forum for discussion, although it was not until 1897 that conferences were established on a regular basis.[12] For the Dominions the main advantage of Imperial Conferences was that they had no power to bind them. Any resolutions passed had to be referred to the respective colonial legislatures before becoming operative. Otherwise, the conferences encouraged free discussion and the airing of views in a club-like atmosphere. Although eventually bodies like the Committee of Imperial Defence serviced the conferences, there was no permanent conference secretariat, and when the delegates dispersed the organs of inter-imperial communication were indentical to those between Britain and foreign powers – the telegraph and the letter.

The use of the term 'Imperial conference' was not decided upon until 1907. Former gatherings had been called 'Colonial Conferences', but in 1905 Lyttelton, the Colonial Secretary, had suggested the title 'Imperial Council'. The final adoption of the term 'Imperial Conference' was something of a triumph for those who wished to emphasise the rather informal and unconventional character of the meetings. The 1907 Imperial Conference also agreed to describe the great self-governing colonies (Canada, Australia, New Zealand and Newfoundland) as 'Dominions', although the Cape, Natal, the Transvaal and the Orange Free State lingered on as 'self-governing colonies' until the Union of 1910.[13]

Such an earnest definition of terms reveals the evolutionary nature of the self-governing Empire, and the determination of colonial governments to get the picture as clear as possible. The classical illustration of this determination came at the 1911 Imperial Conference when Sir Joseph Ward of New Zealand found himself in deep waters with his proposal for an Imperial Parliament of Defence:

> Sir Wilfrid Laurier [Prime Minister of Canada]: But you say 'Council'. Is it a council, or is it a parliament? It is important to know exactly what is the proposal.
> Sir Joseph Ward: I prefer to call it a parliament.
> Sir Wilfrid Laurier: Very good then; now we understand what you mean.
> Sir Joseph Ward: I prefer to call it a parliament, although I admit there is everything in the name.
> Sir Wilfrid Laurier: There is everything in the name.[14]

The growing spirit of Dominion nationalism drew strength from such displays, and after the Conference of 1907 Louis Botha, Prime Minister of the Transvaal, said with some satisfaction of Laurier 'He and I agree about everything.' This was certainly true on the central theme of Dominion development. By 1911 the old choices of centralisation or disintegration were equally inappropriate. What was emerging was a decentralised Commonwealth of white self-governing communities who would co-operate, rather gingerly, in certain agreed areas. Any reforms in organisation had to conform to this situation. Thus the CID and the Dominions Department of the Colonial office were acceptable, while an Imperial Defence Council or a Permanent Commission were not. Chamberlain's proposal to extend the functions of the Judicial Committee of the Privy Council as a Final Court of Appeal for the Empire received a dusty answer. There was to be no setting back of the clock.

In the last resort, therefore, the strongest bonds of Empire were the most natural, the least obstrusive. The monarchy was one such bond. So was a common language, and a common cultural and constitutional identity. Even these links, however, had to be stretched hard in order to incorporate Afrikaners and French Canadians, let alone non-Europeans. There were perhaps two other aids to imperial harmony: common self-interest and international crisis. When war broke out in August 1914 the relations between Britain and her Dominions were, for a time, galvanised.

## SOUTH AFRICA

### Post-war Reconstruction

In May 1902 the Peace of Vereeniging ended the Boer War. British supremacy had been asserted throughout southern Africa. The two Boer republics (the Transvaal and the Orange Free State) had been annexed. A great influx of British capital and British immigrants was anticipated. South Africa's future looked even more golden than before.

In the event, British aspirations were not completely fulfilled. The war had left deep wounds among the Afrikaner people. Memories of farm-burnings and the concentration camps were difficult to exorcise. Reconciliation was of prime importance, therefore, and the Treaty of Vereeniging through its moderately generous financial terms for the defeated, and through its commitment to leave the question of the native franchise to the judgement of the Transvaal and Orange Free State when they became self-governing, certainly aided Anglo-Afrikaner co-operation.

British supremacy, however, was incompatible with whole-hearted reconciliation. Alfred Milner, the High Commissioner from 1898–1905, sought in vain to ensure that the future was secure for British interests. Aided by a group of brilliant young men, known as the 'Milner Kindergarten' (many of whom like L. S. Amery, John Buchan and Lionel Curtis were to have distinguished careers), Milner pressed for the anglicisation of South African institutions.[15] Basically, 'Milnerism' failed. No federation, forced or voluntary, emerged during Milner's term of office, although a customs union, which included Rhodesia, was established in 1903.

There were several reasons for the frustration of Milner's plans. One was the reluctance of the British government to sanction 'federation from above'. That is, forcible federation which would have involved the suspension of the constitution of the self-governing Cape Colony as well as ignoring the wishes of the Afrikaner populations of the Transvaal and the Orange Free State. In addition, Balfour's Unionist administration had been under sentence of death since the 1903 split over tariff reform. Why should Afrikaner leaders voluntarily take part in any federal schemes when, if they waited for the election of a Liberal government in Britain, they might well be granted full self-government?

Milner's final years in South Africa were, therefore, somewhat sterile. Indeed, they provided the British government with the acute embarrassment of the Chinese labour scandal. This arose when the British Cabinet sanctioned the introduction of Chinese coolies into the Rand goldmines in 1904. The object was to fill the gap created by the exodus of much African labour during the Boer War. Many new gold-mining companies had been formed, and it seemed absurd that the industrial Rand (in some ways the chief spoil of war) should not work to full capacity. By 1905 nearly 45,000 coolies had reached the Transvaal, and between 1903 and 1906 gold production doubled.[16]

Rising profits did not, however, still liberal disquiet at the rigorous and restrictive indentured labour system under which the Chinese worked. These misgivings were confirmed by the revelation in 1905 of various abuses, including legalised flogging, in the coolie camps. In Britain, humanitarians condemned 'Chinese slavery' on the Rand. Trade unionists disliked the competition from dirt-cheap, indentured labour. The Liberal party were delighted at yet another opportunity to attack the government, and the Liberal leader, Sir Henry Campbell-Bannerman, pledged himself to end the indentured labour system when he came to office. This pledge was fundamentally honoured when a Liberal administration was formed in December 1905. There is also evidence that the scandal cost the Unionists a substantial number of votes in the general election of January 1906, although it is easy to exaggerate this.[17]

The new Liberal government also announced its intention of speedily granting self-government to the Transvaal and the Orange Free State. The West-Ridgeway Commission was sent to South Africa to thresh out the necessary constitutional changes. Their efforts were naturally concentrated on the Transvaal where there were Afrikaans and English-speaking communities of similar size. After much haggling, an allotment of seats in the new legislature was made. The English-speaking Rand was expected to outvote the rural, Afrikaans-speaking, Transvaal.

In the elections of February 1907 the very opposite happened. The English vote was split between three parties, of which the most important was the Progressive party. The Afrikaner vote was not only proportionally higher (72.5 per cent against 65.1 per cent), but also went solidly to Het Volk (the People's party) which won thirty-seven seats as opposed to the Progressive's twenty-one.[18] Within five years of the victorious conclusion of the Boer War, therefore, Britain has bestowed self-government on the vanquished.

Despite continuing British financial control of the Rand, Milnerism, in the broader sense, now lay in ruins. Although it could be claimed that the Liberal government's action had upheld the best traditions of British colonial policy, this was small comfort for those who hoped for British supremacy. As it happened, events over the next three years were to provide some consolation.

### The Union of South Africa

The Boer War had swept away the old Krugerite leadership of the Afrikaners and replaced it with younger, more liberal, spirits. Dominant among these were Louis Botha (1862–1919) and Jan Christian Smuts (1870–1950). Both men had been brilliantly successful commando generals during the war; both were anxious to encourage Anglo-Afrikaner harmony and the 'Greater South Africa' that might then emerge. Somewhat to their surprise, Botha and Smuts found themselves in 1907 at the head of the new government of the Transvaal.

They were an ideally balanced team. Botha was solid, tactful and dependable; a man of his word. The sort of Prime Minister guaranteed to reassure Rand share-holders. Smuts, with his Cambridge double first, was brilliant and urbane; an internationalist. But he was also something of an intriguer and tactician. His Afrikaans nickname of 'Slim Jannie' ('smart Jannie') was not altogether a compliment. He found compromise easy.

It was Smuts who in 1908 initiated the movement towards a South African Union. In May 1908 representatives of the four self-governing colonies met to consider the renewal of the South African customs union. On the second day of the conference, Smuts proposed that a convention should be appointed to draft a constitution for union. Circumstances were on his side. Not only the government of the Transvaal, but also the leaders of the Cape and the Free State favoured union, although Natal was more hesitant.

By February 1909 a draft constitution was approved. The legislature of the Union was to be at Cape Town, the executive at Pretoria and the judiciary at Bloemfontein. Compromise was the order of the day. Equal language rights and universal European male suffrage were accepted. To satisfy the Transvaal and the Orange Free State, the Cape agreed to the exclusion of non-Europeans from the national parliament, although the limited franchise of coloureds and Africans in the Cape was to be entrenched in the constitution. The future constitutional rights of non-Europeans were, however, likely to be in jeopardy, and the chief radical criticisms in the British House of Commons of the Union of South Africa Act of 1909 were concentrated on this issue.

In 1910 the Union of South Africa was formally established. The Union's first Prime Minister was Botha, whose Cabinet included Smuts and also the more inflexible Afrikaner nationalist Hertzog. In 1912 Hertzog was dropped from the government partly to allay disquiet among English-speaking South Africans, but his career was by no means over.[19] Compromise, indeed, was the hallmark of Botha's administration up to 1914. Given the enormous problems of industrial relations, Anglo-Afrikaner reconciliation, and the future of the non-Europeans, this is perhaps not very surprising. Compromise, however, was usually at the price of the non-European. Before the Act of Union even the British government had waived its traditional concern on such issues. Its reward was a degree of Anglo-Afrikaner co-operation which survived the outbreak of the Great War.

Despite the creation of the Union of South Africa and the optimism that this generated in different parts of the Empire, the omens were, in several ways, misleading.

Though hailed as the 'fourth Dominion', another imperial cub at the side of the old British lion, South Africa was likely to be an awkward recruit to the self-governing empire. The Afrikaner majority among the white population contained many who were bitterly opposed to the imperial connection and for whom the Boer War was still very much alive. Indeed, though South Africa eventually played a full part in the First World War, the declaration of hostilities in August 1914 precipitated an armed rebellion among those Afrikaner die-hards who had no wish to see their country at war with Imperial Germany, their erstwhile, though ineffective, champion.[20]

Even among Afrikaner moderates there was little desire to be seen as unequivocal supporters of the British Empire, and at the Colonial Conferences of 1907 and 1911, Louis Botha sided with Wilfred Laurier of Canada in upholding the cause of imperial devolution.

If the moderate Botha–Smuts axis wished to keep the 'imperial factor' at a respectable distance, the Nationalist leader Hertzog wanted to rid South Africa of the spectre once and for all. After his accession to power in 1924 he was at last given the opportunity to carry out this aim.

All of this helped to make South Africa a markedly different Dominion from Australia and New Zealand, and even from Canada, before 1914. There was as yet no Irish Free State, no 'Irish Botha', to pursue similar objectives.

South Africa's potentially intractable racial problem also set her aside from the other Dominions. Though most Edwardian observers tended to diagnose the South African 'race question' as one concerning Afrikaners and British, the future relationship between white and non-white was destined to be by far the more forbidding and intractable. The liberal hope, cherished in Britain at the making of the Union of South Africa, that the less repressive official racial attitudes of the Cape would somehow miraculously convert the hard-line Transvaal and Orange Free State was soon shown to be a brittle illusion.

## CANADA, AUSTRALIA AND NEW ZEALAND, 1902–14. SOME DOMESTIC THEMES

### Canada

As well as being the eldest daughter state of the self-governing Empire, Canada was arguably the most awkward. This was chiefly due to her uncertain international identity and her domestic tensions.

On the world stage, Canada was neither fully British nor fully North American. Politically and economically she provided (sometimes to her own discomfiture) the third point of a triangular relationship between Great Britain, the United States and herself. While Canada could occasionally use this position to her advantage, if the two great powers chose to co-operate they could deliberately ignore her interests. This happened when Britain abandoned Canada's claims during the Alaska border dispute of 1903.[21] Nor was the attempt to found a Canadian navy as successful as some had hoped. The two Navy Bills of 1909 and 1912 were mauled in Parliament, and when war broke out in 1914 Canada possessed only two frigates which at once passed under the control of Britain.

In other fields, however, Canada was able to assert herself as a more or less independent nation. This was nowhere more true than in commercial matters. As early as 1879 the British government had agreed that Canada could contract out of British commercial treaties. Canada had in the meantime waged a trade war with Germany, and in 1907 negotiated a commercial treaty with France (although the British government insisted that their representative should countersign the treaty). A reciprocity treaty with the United States followed in 1908.

In the period 1901 to 1911 the Canadian population rose from 5,371,315 to 7,206,643, an increase of nearly 35 per cent.[22] The prairie provinces benefited most from this new migration and Alberta and Saskatchewan saw their populations spectacularly augmented. A significant characteristic of the movement of emigrants to Canada between 1901 to 1911 lay in the fact that large numbers now came from Russia (including the Ukraine), the Austrian Empire, Germany and Poland. In 1901, indeed, emigrants from Britain and France accounted for only 30 per cent of the total intake; 70 per cent came from less traditional sources. This shift in emigration patterns meant that by 1911 the ratio of British and French to the rest in the total population was only 83 per cent compared with 92 per cent in 1871.[23]

All this meant that flesh was being put on to the bones of the Dominion of Canada, even though not all the parts of the body yet functioned smoothly. Above all, it was necessary to invest confidence in the Canadian future. The Liberal Prime Minister Wilfrid Laurier did just that when he declared that the twentieth century would belong to Canada. When, in 1911, the Laurier government fell and Robert Borden's Conservatives took over, their picture of Canada's role in imperial and international matters was equally optimistic. The senior Dominion would continue to assert her seniority.

*Australia, 1902–14*

The period 1901–14 saw the new Australian federation at work. One of the first preoccupations of the Commonwealth government, led by the Liberal Prime Minister Edmund Barton, was with immigration. More than 95 per cent of the 4,000,000 citizens of Australia were of British extraction. Following the examples of the previous state governments it now became the policy of the central government to ensure that immigration restrictions were maintained. An Act passed in 1901 required intending coloured immigrants to pass a test in any prescribed European language. This meant in practice any language which the prospective immigrant did *not* know – thus Chinese could be required to speak Swedish, or Indians to have a working knowledge of Portuguese!

The 'White Australia' policy had the backing of all the major parties and of the overwhelming majority of the population. Still relatively insecure on the edge of the Asian land mass, Australians viewed heavy coloured immigration with trepidation, and contemplated the social consequences of such an influx with distaste. The determination to maintain Anglo-Saxon cultural and political traditions was deep-rooted, yet between 1901 and 1906 Australia had a net loss of population of 17,000 through substantial emigration, and it became necessary for some of the major states to restore immigration assistance. The years 1911–14, however, saw a heartening increase in immigrants from Britain, even though the post-war crop was on average disappointing.[24]

But it was the tariff controversy, not immigration, that divided Australian politicians in the first years of the new federation. The 1901 election had been fought chiefly over the tariff issue. The protectionists won, and formed the Liberal government; the free trade Conservatives went into opposition. Prime Minister Barton introduced a compromise tariff in 1902; this had the effect of protecting certain industries while making a concession to British exporters possible. Barton's search for a compromise position between the embattled forces of free-traders and protectionists had its contemporary parallel in Britain where the Prime Minister, A. J. Balfour, attempted an unsatisfactory balancing act between similar extremes from 1903–5.

In 1908, largely on the insistence of the pro-Chamberlain, protectionist Prime Minister Alfred Deakin, the Australian government introduced a preference of 5 per cent on British goods. Although Britain was not in a position to offer reciprocal preferences with a staunchly free trade Liberal administration in power, the door was now open for some future trade agreement.

Perhaps the 1908 tariff would have been impossible without Deakin's leadership. Certainly he was the dominating political figure of the first decade of the new federation. He led three administrations between 1901 and 1910: that of 1903–4 as a Liberal, with Labour support; from 1905–8, again with Labour backing; and from 1909–10 as the leader of a coalition of anti-Labour parties. With his background of the law and journalism, the eloquent, immaculate and persuasive Deakin was an impressive personality not only in Australia but within the wider imperial context.[25]

Apart from the tariff question, defence was a major consideration of the new Commonwealth. Acutely aware of the rising power of Japan, and of German activities in the South Seas, Australia proposed at the Imperial Conference of 1907 that she should establish a small naval squadron of her own. The great 'navy scare' of 1909, sparked off by the rapid progress of the German naval programme, led to an Imperial Defence Conference in London in the same year. It was now agreed that an Australian squadron should be formed and that Australia should mainly finance and maintain this squadron. By 1914 a small Royal Australian Navy did exist, but as previously arranged was put under the central authority of the British admiralty.

The Australian Navy was brought into being under the Labour Prime Minister, Andrew Fisher. Indeed the accession of Labour to power (in 1904, 1908–9, and 1910–13) was one of the most remarkable aspects of pre-war Australian politics, and a significant augury for both Britain and New Zealand. Fisher's Scots hard-headedness, reliability and moderation won him widespread respect and gave the Australian Labour movement a distinctly non-revolutionary flavour.

The early Labour governments achieved a considerable legislative output. They improved the welfare schemes introduced by the Deakin government in 1908, so that by 1913 Australia had old age and invalid pensions, and maternity allowances. A State Commonwealth Bank was set up. Fisher also tried to give the federal government legal power to intervene in industrial disputes and monopolies over the head of the High Court and the Arbitration Court. In this he failed. But when the Great War broke out in August 1914, coinciding with a general election, Labour was returned to power for the fourth time since 1901.

## New Zealand, 1902–14

For much of this period the New Zealand economy remained buoyant. The year 1895 had seen a significant rise in the value of exports, and this trend was maintained in the early years of the new century, reaching a peak between 1904 and 1907. Wool, meat and dairy produce were New Zealand's chief money-earners. Here, as in other fields, the progress was gratifying. In 1911 the value of exported wool was about £6,500,000, in 1916 about £12,500,000; in 1911 dairy and meat exports were worth some £6,000,000, in 1916 some £13,500,000.[26]

In 1907, however, there was a 25 per cent drop in export income due mainly to a financial crisis in Britain and the United States. The New Zealand economy took this blow with far more resilience than it had exhibited under Julius Vogel in the 1880s. The advent of refrigerated ships made it very likely that the export of meat and dairy produce would continue to increase overall. Moreover, between 1891 and 1906 there had been substantial budget surpluses. As a reflection of economic self-confidence the Auckland to Wellington main trunk railway was opened in 1908, and the state then gave more financial aid to local projects for road and railway building.

The Liberal party continued in power until 1912. Drawing on

small farmer and worker support, it was led, until 1906, by the towering figure of Richard Seddon. Canny, homely and direct, Dick Seddon did not pretend to be a man of culture. His enemies indeed claimed that he had never read a book in his life, but his friends denied this and insisted that he had read at least one! Seddon had begun as miners' representative, became the architect of New Zealand's welfare state while in office, and ended as an ardent imperialist.

In the sphere of public welfare New Zealand led the whole of the English-speaking world. It has been suggested that the enfranchisement of women in 1893 (a quarter of a century before women over thirty in Britain) prompted Seddon to introduce legislation that would especially appeal to these new voters. However this may be, the Old Age Pension Act of 1898, the encouragement of a free, secular and compulsory national education system, and the Public Health Act of 1900 were great achievements. Attempts were made to provide effective machinery for conciliating employers and employees in industrial disputes.

Joseph Ward succeeded Seddon as Prime Minister in 1906. Ward lacked Seddon's astute touch, and his tenure of office (until 1912) was relatively uncomfortable. The chief problems were those of land reform and industrial unrest. At the 1911 General Election the Reform party, led by W. F. Massey, drew level with the Liberals; four Independent Labour members were also elected. Ward struggled on as premier for seven months, but in July 1912 Massey came to power. The Reform party drew its strength from urban businessmen and North Island farmers. Massey was himself a farmer. He was to remain Prime Minister until 1925.

The new administration inherited serious labour problems. The United Labour party was formed in 1912 and, although it by no means united the labour movement, it began to drain support from the Liberals, especially from the Liberal-Labour section of the party. A series of bitter disputes, including the Waihi miners' strike of May 1912, led to a basically unsuccessful general strike in November 1913. The unions lacked cohesion, and the government (backed by the special police, known as 'Massey's cossacks') stood firm. In 1916 the New Zealand Labour party was founded, and trade union leaders could now use this increasingly powerful political weapon with great effect. The ballot box, rather than strike action, seemed the more appropriate means of progress.

## THE INDIAN EMPIRE, 1902–14

This period of Indian history was marked by two phenomena. One was the viceroyalty of Lord Curzon, the other was the unprecedented growth of Indian nationalism. Curzon's term as Viceroy lasted from 1898 to 1905, and can be seen as the apotheosis of the Raj in India. Curzon brought to his daunting task as the ruler of nearly 300,000,000 subjects boundless energy and unlimited self-assurance. High-minded and thorough, he embodied some of the best qualities of the Indian Civil Service.

Unfortunately Curzon was also arrogant, obstinate and petty. His impatience and ill-concealed contempt tended to alienate colleagues. He considered that no Indian was fitted to high office in his own land.[27] Convinced that the British government did not appreciate his problems and his policies, he sought, on several occasions, to outwit the Cabinet in London. Curzon could only see India within the context of British Imperial interests. This meant that he applied criteria that were occasionally misleading (even offensive) to peculiarly Indian matters.

On the positive side, Curzon flung himself into a vigorous reform of certain aspects of Indian administration and life. He established a new famine policy, improved the railway system, and encouraged agricultural innovation and irrigation schemes. He strove, within limits, to better the Indian education system. Moreover, he insisted that the Raj must show no discrimination between Europeans and Indians in cases brought before the courts. In three instances, his determined intervention brought Europeans to justice in cases involving outrages committed against Indians. His championship of legal equality won him firm support from much of the Indian press and from informed Indian opinion. Moreover, it was very clearly an expression of Curzon's conviction that the Raj must be seen to be purer and more just than any other rule could be.[28] Curzon's domestic policies provoked little criticism in Whitehall compared with his initiatives on the frontiers of India. Extensive travels in Asia before he became Viceroy had convinced him that Russian expansion posed the gravest threat to British interests throughout the continent. He therefore wanted to turn the Persian Gulf into a 'British lake', and to extend influence over southern Persia. In addition, Afghanistan and Tibet seemed to him to be areas which must be cleared of Russian influence.

Once he became Viceroy, Curzon set about implementing this

'forward policy'. In Persia and the Gulf his ambitions were already in process of fulfilment. But the British government at home had no desire for unnecessary, and expensive, entanglements in Afghanistan and Tibet. The Anglo-Japanese alliance of 1902 had provided a powerful watchdog for Britain's Asian interests. By 1904, moreover, the Balfour administration (1902–5) had come to an agreement with Russia over their mutual concern in buffer states like Tibet and Afghanistan; both sides promised to practise non-intervention.

Curzon, however, believed wholeheartedly in the Russian threat. He therefore planned to outmanoeuvre the Cabinet in London with masterly and independent action. He pressed for a more exacting treaty arrangement with the Amir of Afghanistan, and was incensed when the British government preferred to continue with a more informal understanding. In the case of Tibet, Curzon obtained the somewhat grudging permission of the Balfour administration to send a mission to Lhasa to negotiate a trade treaty. This was an apparently inoffensive, even profitable, project. But Curzon transformed the mission into a fully-fledged invasion.

Led by Colonel Younghusband, the invasion force left its base in December 1903. By the middle of 1904 it had fought its way into the forbidden city of Lhasa. There terms were dictated which far exceeded the wishes of the Cabinet. In particular there was objection to the occupation of the strategically important Chumbi Valley against an indemnity payable over seventy-five years. Believing that Younghusband had wilfully ignored his instructions, the government vetoed this clause in the treaty and substituted a milder, three-year indemnity. Curzon's hopes of a *fait accompli* were dashed, and the principle that the governments of Britain and India should pursue joint foreign policies had been usefully reasserted.[29]

Curzon's viceregal career would have survived this signal rebuff, despite the illusory nature of Russian influence in Tibet, and despite the deception involved in mounting the expedition. But the Viceroy became involved in a histrionic and acrimonious quarrel with Kitchener of Khartoum, Commander-in-Chief of the Indian Army from 1902–9. Basically the quarrel centred on Kitchener's desire to abolish the Military Member of the Viceroy's Council, a permanent official with oversight of supply and spending. Curzon raised the spectre of military autocracy; Kitchener complained that the existence of the Military Member hindered the army's efficiency. There was something in both arguments. Eventually the British

government, chary of overriding a Commander-in-Chief of
Kitchener's reputation, refused to support Curzon.

After some dramatic entreaties, Curzon resigned in August 1905.
His paramount aim as Viceroy had been to ensure that India
remained a loyal member of the Empire into the forseeable future.
Ironically he left India reverberating to a fierce controversy over
the 1905 partition of Bengal. Though justifiable on administrative
grounds, the partition antagonised many of the Bengali people –
who were among the most politically active and sophisticated of the
Indian population. The Indian Congress, dismissed by Curzon in
1900 as 'tottering to its fall' found a powerful cause. Indian
nationalist agitation had begun in earnest.[30]

Of all her imperial possessions, Britain could least afford to lose
India. One-fifth of British overseas investment was sunk in India –
nearly £300,000,000 by the beginning of the twentieth century.
Furthermore, 19 per cent of Britain's exports were taken by India.
The Indian Army, paid for by the Indian taxpayer, was an
invaluable source of imperial military strength. If India, the
keystone of the Empire, was removed, then the justification for
holding other territories would sharply decrease. For all these
reasons, and perhaps for the less tangible prestige generated by the
imposing structure of the Raj, British governments did not view
Indian nationalism with relish.

Indian nationalist feeling, however, was growing fast during the
Edwardian era. The controversy over Curzon's partition of Bengal
gave a platform to the more radical members of Congress. By 1906
there were two groups battling for the control of Congress. The
extremists led by Tilak advocated a nationwide boycott of British
goods and British administration. Tilak's followers believed that
any settlement short of real independence (*Swaraj*) would be a
sham. The moderates were led by Gokhale who argued that
eventual self-government within the Empire was possible due to the
democratic principles that were the fabric of the British political
system. Antagonism between the two factions led to the suspension
of the 1907 Congress amid scenes of considerable disorder. At the
1908 Congress the extremists (or Nationalists) were excluded.[31]

The new militancy of Congress was accompanied by the growth
of Muslim separatism. In 1906 the Muslim League was founded to
give political expression to the discontent and grievances of India's
Muslim minority. These developments had their effect on the
Morley–Minto Reforms of 1907–9. Morley (the Liberal Secretary

of State for India from 1905-12) and Lord Minto (Conservative Viceroy from 1905-10) were at first sight unlikely partners in the cause of reform. But both wanted to save the Raj. Minto wanted to prop up loyal and conservative elements in India; Morley, a cautious Gladstonian, believed that Indian welfare depended on continuing British rule.[32]

The Morley–Minto Reforms fell into two categories. First, two Indians were admitted to the Secretary of State's India Council in London, and one Indian each to the Viceroy's Executive Council and to the Governors' Executive Councils. Second, the India Councils Act (1909) expanded the Indian Legislative Councils. Although these measures aroused hostility among Conservative elements in Britain, and among the white community in India, they were not as radical as their critics claimed.

The Indians appointed to the various councils were moderates rather than revolutionaries. The key appointment to the Viceroy's Council went to S. P. Sinha, whom Minto preferred to the other potential appointee on the grounds that 'Sinha is comparatively white, whilst Mookerjee is as black as my hat!'[33] The expansion of the central and provincial Legislative Council introduced communal representation (a clear victory for Minto and for the Muslim League), as well as representation for landlords and chambers of commerce. It was unlikely that Indian nationalists would be satisfied by these measures. It was also now evident that the future contest for power in India would involve three parties: the British, Congress, and the Muslim League.

## THE COLONIAL EMPIRE, 1902-14

In 1902 the Colonial Empire was widely divergent in character, and by no means uniformly profitable. The Caribbean colonies were mostly venerable members of the Empire, but now destitute and backward. In the Mediterranean, Gibraltar, Malta, Cyprus and Egypt, were necessary to the logistics of naval supremacy and the safeguarding of the route to India. Egypt, in addition, had increasing commercial value; this was not true of Gibraltar or Malta.

Britain's African colonies offered some commercial pickings. Between 1911 and 1914 British West Africa had a total overseas trade of £26,418,000: mostly in agricultural products like palm oil, hardwoods, and cocoa, but also in gold and ivory. In Central Africa, Nyasaland was of no special value, although Southern Rhodesia was expanding its agricultural activities, and Northern Rhodesia's copper deposits were eventually to make it one of the most profitable of Britain's African possessions. The East African territories of Kenya, Uganda, Somaliland, Zanzibar and the Sudan were generally of little economic value, although some hope was invested in Ugandan cotton as well as in the European farmers of Kenya's 'White Highlands'.

The Indian Ocean territories, like Mauritius, the Seychelles, Aden and the Persian Gulf protectorates, were of continuing strategic importance. The Gulf protectorates, moreover, were soon to be coveted for their oil deposits. Ceylon was another colony originally acquired for its naval base (at Trincomalee); commercially Ceylon's production of tea made little difference to Britain's trading position. This was not true of the Malay states, providing tin and rubber, nor of Borneo, which also produced rubber as well as oil.

The islands of Hong Kong and Singapore were the booming entrepôts of Britain's eastern trade. The Pacific islands of Fiji, Tonga, Gilbert and Ellice, for example, were nothing of the sort. Indeed, Britain's Pacific possessions could hardly be justified on the grounds of commerce or strategy. Later it seemed expedient to allow Australia and New Zealand to take over the administration of certain islands.

A good proportion of the colonial empire, therefore, was of no direct value to Britain, though a number of individual businessmen found that the colonies offered scope for financial gain. National needs had altered since the acquisition of many of these territories. But it was not possible for the British government to cut its losses and abandon useless possessions. Pre-1914 international rivalry rendered such self-sacrifice impossible. In any case, the intense reluctance of the British treasury to subsidise ailing colonies reduced expenditure – though an exception had been made in the case of the West Indies after the report of the Norman Commission in 1897.

In the decade before the Great War, the British government even managed to promote a certain uniformity in the colonial empire. Protectorates, protected states and some chartered territories were gradually assimilated to Crown Colony status. Exceptions to this process were widespread, and probably unavoidable, but by 1914 much had been achieved. Subordination to British imperial interests was combined with the potential for substantial local autonomy.

In Africa, Lugard's concept of 'indirect rule' gave further expression to this formula. Based on his experiences in Northern Nigeria, Lugard's policy sought to combine the traditional oversight of the imperial power with the retention and development of indigenous institutions. Thus local chieftains, though subordinated to the larger aims of British policy, were encouraged to run their own treasuries and law courts. Variants of 'indirect rule' spread to other parts of Africa, and lent some uniformity to British policy towards indigenous peoples.[34]

'Indirect Rule' had the merit of being cheap to administer. It also seemed to preserve native society from destruction at the hands of white officialdom. Humanitarians, anthropologists and civil servants could therefore agree as to its value. Unfortunately, 'indirect rule' often served, in the long run, merely to entrench much that was rigidly conservative in tribal society. In this sense it did a disservice to African progress, in that it tended to provoke conflict between these conservative elements and those nationalists who subsequently pursued the goal of modernisation.

## THE EMPIRE AT WAR

Britain's declaration of war in August 1914 committed the whole Empire to the hostilities. The Dominions accepted this fact in different ways. The Australian Prime Minister, Joseph Cook, said 'Australia is part of the Empire. When the Empire is at war, so is Australia at war'.[35] New Zealand acted upon similar convictions. The Canadian government, and the Liberal opposition, also accepted their nation's involvement in the struggle, though Laurier (the Liberal leader) emphasised that the extent of this involvement was a decision for the Dominions alone. The infant navies of Canada and Australia were put at the disposal of the British Admiralty.

In the Union of South Africa the response to war was more ambiguous. Pro-German and anti-British feeling among a section of the Afrikaner people led to a not inconsiderable rebellion. The rising was crushed by the ex-Boer War generals Louis Botha (the Prime Minister) and Jan Smuts (Minister for Defence). Even the Irish Nationalist MPs at Westminster indicated their support for the

Asquith government, and thousands of Irishmen from the southern counties volunteered for active service. In India the extreme nationalists did not oppose the war, and more conservative elements supported it wholeheartedly.

The statistics of the war effort (including the percentage of the adult male population) are impressive enough. Britain recruited 6,704,416 men (22.11 per cent) of whom 704,803 died. Canada recruited 628,964 men, of whom 458,218 (13.48 per cent) served overseas; 56,639 lost their lives. Australia recruited 412,953 men and sent overseas 331,814 (13.43 per cent), of whom 59,330 died. New Zealand recruited 128,525 men, sending 112,223 (19.55 per cent) overseas; 16,711 were killed or died of wounds. South Africa recruited 136,070 whites, sending 76,184 abroad (11.12 per cent), of whom 7121 died. Over 8000 Newfoundlanders served overseas, of whom 1204 lost their lives.[36]

The non-European Empire also contributed handsomely to a war that was mostly far-removed from their immediate interests. 1,440,437 men volunteered for the Indian army, of whom 62,056 died. British East Africa raised some 34,000 fighting troops, losing about 2000; the British West African colonies raised 25,000 men, of whom 850 died. Tens of thousands from other possessions served in non-combatant units: 82,000 Egyptians; 8000 West Indians; 1000 Mauritians, and even 100 from Fiji.[37]

These forces, mostly financed from their own treasuries, fought throughout the globe. South Africans conquered South West Africa and Tanganyika; Canadians died in their thousands in Flanders; Australians and New Zealanders played a substantial part in the ill-fated Gallipoli campaign; Indian troops invaded Mesopotamia. It really did seem as if the British Empire had rallied as never before to meet its greatest test.

Yet the progress of the war revealed fundamental problems and divergencies within the Empire. French Canada supported the war with far less enthusiasm than English-speaking Canada, and the conscription crisis in 1917 resulted in severe civil disorder in Quebec. In Dublin, at Easter 1916, the republican rebellion heralded widespread disaffection and the beginning of the last violent struggle for home rule. Even in patriotic Australia conscription was put to the vote in a referendum – and defeated.

Indian loyalty at the outbreak of war had given way by 1916 to a renewal of demands for self-rule. Both loyalty and agitation prompted the British government to consider new reforms. The

Liberal Edwin Montagu became Secretary of State for India in 1917 and declared in the House of Commons for 'the progressive realisation of responsible government in India as an integral part of the British Empire'.[38] Montagu visited India in November 1917 and conferred with the Viceroy (Lord Chelmsford), and also with Tilak and Jinnah (the Muslim leader).

Impressed with the problems of Indian political development, Montagu produced with Chelmsford a report in 1918. The Montagu–Chelmsford reforms were given expression in the Government of India Act of 1919. As a result, provincial legislatures had their elective elements enlarged and provincial governments were to be appointed on the principle of dyarchy whereby European ministers retained certain vital portfolios (police, justice and land revenue), while Indian ministers became responsible for departments like education, public health and public works. A central legislature of 146 members was also created. Although central government remained authoritarian, semi-democracy had come to the provinces.[39] Unfortunately the Rowlatt Acts with their repressive provisions against sedition, and the tragic massacre at Amritsar in 1919, made it difficult for Indian nationalists to treat the new measures with an open mind.

The Dominions were also able to assert their national needs as a result of the war. The Imperial War Conference of 1917, while appearing to be the high watermark of imperial co-operation, was also the occasion for the Dominion leaders to press for an Imperial Conference after the war to adjust the constitutional relations of the self-governing Empire. In a word, to define Dominion status in realistic terms.[40]

This was perfectly reasonable. So was the subsequent request of the Dominions to be admitted as independent nations to the Peace Conferences, and to be able to sign the peace treaties in their own right.[41] After all, merely in terms of their war effort it would have been ludicrous to deny Canada and Australia the diplomatic position enjoyed by states like Belgium and Portugal. The Dominions, therefore, were represented as separate nations at the Peace Conferences, as well as being part of the British Empire delegations (despite French suspicions of 'conference packing'). India, too, was allowed to sign the treaties in her own right, though this was a less meaningful concession in view of India's lack of self-governing status.

By 1919, therefore, the Dominions had been seen to 'come of

age' – both in a practical and in a diplomatic sense – something which Lloyd George's decision to treat them (and India) as equals at the 1917 Imperial Conference had ensured. Their membership of the League of Nations, and, in the case of Australia, New Zealand and South Africa, their acquisition of mandated territories, was further proof of this. But such developments, and the growing crisis in India and Ireland, were apparent contradictions to the unprecedented wartime centralisation of imperial activities. The British Prime Minister, David Lloyd George, hoped to continue the spirit of co-operation and the practice of centralisation into the post-war era, but the real portents were those of disintegration, not of unity.

# PART 3

# THE EMPIRE/COMMONWEALTH
# AT PEACE, 1919–39

## THE HEYDAY OF THE COLONIAL EMPIRE, 1919–39

By 1939, it was evident that the imperial system could not long continue to resist the pressure of Indian nationalism. Other concessions to local national sentiment were also made during this period: in Ireland, to which Dominion status was conceded in 1921; in Egypt, where the British unilaterally terminated the short-lived protectorate in 1922; and in Ceylon, where a form of responsible government was introduced in 1931. Were these developments symptomatic of growth or decay? Perhaps it is as much a distortion of history to see them as signs of imperial decline as to accept the view (still widely held in the interim period) that the British Empire would endure as long as the Roman Empire had done.

In 1919 the Empire reached its widest extent as a result of the acquisition of a clutch of 'mandated territories' from the newly created League of Nations. Basically the colonial possessions of defeated Turkey and Germany were shared out among those of the victorious powers who had retained an appetite for colonial acquisitions. Annexation, however, was not in fashion, so the territories were handed over as a 'sacred trust of civilization'. Britain acquired Palestine and some other rather troublesome responsibilities in the Middle East, and rounded off her African Empire with Tanganyika and parts of Togoland and the Cameroons.

1919 was thus the culmination of a generation of rapid territorial expansion, particularly in Africa. In many respects, the following generation was a period of confident consolidation and development in which a whole philosophy of colonial rule was perfected. Moreover, some of the apparently worthless strips of territory acquired during the 'scramble' at the end of the nineteenth century turned out, like Northern Rhodesia, to be rich in vital natural resources.

In India it appeared that the imperial sun was waning, with the government forced to parley with native 'agitators', and with the morale of many British residents affected by the Indianisation of the army, business and the Indian Civil Service. Indeed after the First World War the ICS, once the élite corps of the Empire, found it difficult to obtain its quota of recruits from Britain. In Africa, on the other hand, new imperial energies were being released. Eager Colonial Service recruits set out to sit at the feet of Cameron, Mitchell and other apostles of Lugard's gospel of 'indirect rule'. The Colonial Service thus replaced the ICS as the 'favourite career for young paternalists from Eton and Oxford'.[1] Settlers, many of them veterans of the First World War, set out to build new white dominions in the 'empty' spaces of Kenya or the Rhodesias. Businessmen, alive to Britain's desperate need of new markets and cheap raw materials in increasingly competitive world conditions, gave more serious attention to the resources of the tropical dependencies. It may seem curious to emphasise dynamic elements in the imperial scene when in many places 'development' – to use the modern term – was either non-existent or painfully slow, and when in the West Indies, for example, many of the islands were condemned to economic and social stagnation. Yet, in the minds of many participants, this period remains the tranquil high noon of the Empire.

### Crisis, 1919–22

There was nothing tranquil about the immediate post-war years. The ministers of the Lloyd George coalition were burdened by simultaneous crises arising out of Britain's old and new imperial responsibilities. Although the power of Congress in India was contained despite the rise of Gandhi and the impact of the Amritsar massacre, in the case of Ireland, the oldest 'colonial' problem of all, a kind of settlement was patched up in 1921. In the Middle East, revolts in Egypt and Iraq were suppressed, while at the same time attempts were made to conciliate local nationalism in a way compatible with vital British interests. Thus, in 1922, the new mandate of Iraq obtained self-rule subject to British 'advice', and the protectorate of Egypt was declared 'independent'. A British military presence remained in both countries.

Lord Milner performed his last major public service by going to

Egypt in 1919, heading a mission which recommended the termination of the protectorate; an ironic end to the career of a great proconsul who had fought so hard to establish imperial authority in South Africa after the Boer War. However, the 1922 unilateral declaration of Egyptian independence (by the British!) left severe limitations of Egyptian sovereignty.[2] It was not until 1936 that an Anglo-Egyptian treaty, originally recommended by Milner in 1920, gave some real substance to Egypt's independence.

If relatively conciliatory in Egypt and Iraq, Britain was still prepared, in the immediate post-war period, to deal ruthlessly with lesser manifestations of local 'nationalism'. Thus in Somaliland, the generation-old resistance of the 'Mad Mullah', as Sheikh Mohammed bin Abdullah Hassan was known to the British, was ended by the use of the RAF, then believed to be the cheapest and most effective means of keeping desert tribesmen in order.

### Africa: settlers, indirect rule and development

During the years of immediate post-war crisis, British attention was often diverted from what we might call the colonial Empire proper. Thus, the two Colonial Secretaries of that period, Milner (1919–21) and Winston Churchill (1921–22), were heavily involved in matters strictly outside their departmental responsibilities: Milner with Egypt, Churchill with Ireland. Africa however was soon to recapture something of the limelight enjoyed in the days of the 'scramble' and the Anglo-Boer war.

British attention was first centred on Kenya colony, as the East African Protectorate became known in 1920. The crisis concerned the rival political aspirations of the European and Indian settler minority communities, and posed important questions of imperial policy. The European settlers, under the flamboyant leadership of Lord Delamere and with influential support in Conservative circles in Britain, looked forward to the establishment of a white dominion in East Africa. They wanted to create a 'distinctly British' version of South Africa, with responsible government exclusively in European hands. This would also guarantee the continued social and economic supremacy of the Europeans, involving the reservation of the best land in the so-called 'White Highlands' for their use alone, and a free hand in the exploitation of African labour.

The local Indians, who in 1921 outnumbered the 10,000 Europeans by over 2:1, and who also were mainly recent immigrants, demanded several things: equality with the Europeans; a common roll for elections to the local Legislative Council; the abolition of segregation of residential and commercial areas, and access to the White Highlands. In India itself, this struggle against anti-Indian discrimination in Africa was regarded as a test of imperial good faith. Indeed, the government of India sought to associate itself with Indian grievances.[3]

Pressure from the European and Indian lobbies roused those who were concerned to protect the interests of the vast majority of the Kenyan population – the two and a half million African 'native' inhabitants. The Africans themselves lacked the means to exert effective political pressure, although Harry Thuku organised the Young Kikuyu Association in 1921 to protest against increased taxation and the compulsory carrying of identity cards by adult African males. Thuku was arrested in 1922 and twenty-five Africans were killed in disturbances in Nairobi.

However, missionaries, supported by Church leaders in Britain, took it upon themselves to defend 'native' interests in the Kenya battle. This influential religious lobby was sustained by those like Lord Lugard, the former Governor-General of Nigeria, who believed that in the tropical territories of Africa Britain was a trustee on behalf of the Africans, and that any transfer of political power to minority communities would be a betrayal of that trust.

Indian and European settler leaders now vied with each other in expressing their concern for the protection of African interests, and the 'Devonshire Declaration' of 1923 committed the British government to the view that those interests must be paramount in an African territory such as Kenya and should prevail in any conflict with the interests of the immigrant races.[4]

The Europeans in fact won a limited victory over the Indians, who did not get their common electoral roll. In the long term, however, the doctrine of paramountcy presented a major obstacle to the political aspirations of the Kenya Europeans. If Britain was exercising on behalf of the Africans a trust which she could not delegate, then, said Devonshire (Churchill's successor as Colonial Secretary), the grant of responsible self-government was 'out of the question within any period of time which need now be taken into consideration'. As Elspeth Huxley put it, the Europeans:

> had rubbed the magic lamp of native interests but the Djinn who suddenly materialised before them was an unprepossessing

monster with a nasty look, not at all the obedient servant they had hoped to see.[5]

If trusteeship and the paramountcy of African interests now appeared to be the watchwords for British colonial policy in Africa, the European settlers and their supporters did not abandon the quest for political power. In the same year as the Devonshire Declaration, the settlers in Southern Rhodesia achieved the cherished goal of responsible government. On this occasion the whites had the enthusiastic support of the local missionaries, who believed that 'settler democracy' would serve the interests of the Africans better than the administration of the British South Africa Company which ran the territory under the loosest imperial supervision until 1923.

The ratio of whites to blacks in Southern Rhodesia was a 'mere' 1:25 as compared with 1:250 in Kenya, and there was no Indian complication. The real contrast with Kenya however was the weakness of the 'imperial factor'. Under Company rule, the Rhodesian settlers had gained an elected majority in the local legislature, and had been conceded the right to determine their own political future. Their choice, in a referendum held in 1922, of responsible government rather than union with South Africa left Britain with a theoretical responsibility. In practice, however, the settlers had gained a free hand to proceed with discriminatory racial measures such as the Land Apportionment Act of 1930, which proved a bitter disappointment to those missionaries and humanitarians who had placed their faith in 'settler democracy'.

In effect a 'white dominion' had been created in the heart of Africa. Southern Rhodesia was now free of the 'government by bureaucracy' so detested by the settlers in Kenya and those of Northern Rhodesia where Colonial Office rule had replaced that of the British South Africa Company in 1924. As the paramountcy doctrine apparently stood in the way of these European groups in their quest for the status now enjoyed by the white Rhodesians, it was inevitable that strenuous efforts would be made to undermine it. Thus, as one historian has put it, there commenced a long and bitter controversy over the definition of paramountcy 'comparable in intensity with the debates that used to rage over the details of obscure theological doctrines in ancient Byzantium'.[6]

The settlers came closest to success while Leopold Amery was Colonial Secretary in Baldwin's Conservative government, 1925–9.

Amery, a disciple of Milner and passionate believer in British imperialism, looked forward to the establishment of an East African dominion which would incorporate Kenya, Uganda and Tanganyika and in which the settlers would play the dominant political role. Meanwhile, local Europeans would be associated with the 'high and honourable' task of trusteeship of the African population.

Sir Edward Grigg, Amery's appointee as Governor of Kenya and a strong supporter of local European political ambitions, concocted a scheme for a federation which fitted in with Amery's ideas. Amery's Cabinet colleagues, however, hesitated and appointed a commission under Sir Edward Hilton Young to examine the whole question of closer union of the British territories in east and central Africa. Indian and missionary interests were strongly represented on the commission which brushed aside European settler political aspirations and saw the co-ordination of native policy under a High Commissioner as the first priority of any closer union scheme. The settlers' magic lamp had failed them again.

The fate of Amery's scheme was apparently sealed by the resignation of the Conservative government shortly after the Hilton Young Commission reported in 1929. A Labour minority government took office with the veteran Fabian Sidney Webb (now Lord Passfield) as Colonial Secretary. In two 'black papers' of 1930 the government returned to the purity of the Devonshire Declaration, rejecting the notion that their duties as trustees could ever be handed over to European settlers. Responsible government could only come when every section of the population could find an adequate voice in the electorate.

Settler fury knew no bounds, and the Labour minority government, increasingly preoccupied with the economic crisis at home, was in a weak position to resist Conservative demands for some further modification of the paramountcy doctrine. Eventually a joint select committee of both Houses of Parliament spent almost a year in reconsidering the question of closer union in East Africa. The committee had a Conservative majority, including Amery and his former Under-Secretary, William Ormsby-Gore. But the depression year of 1931 was not the best time for launching schemes of the type which Amery wanted. Closer union was shelved, but the committee's report made concessions to the Europeans in reviving the 'dual policy' of settler and Colonial Office trusteeship and redefining the doctrine of paramountcy as meaning:

no more than that the interests of the overwhelming majority of the indigenous population should not be subordinated to those of a minority belonging to another race, however important in itself.[7]

This negative definition was open to the interpretation that the interests of the non-native population would equally not be subordinated to those of the African native majority in the central and east African territories. There was now room for a considerable difference of emphasis between the Colonial Office at home and colonial governors who sympathised with European settler aspirations. Thus in the 1930s schemes for the amalgamation of the three central African territories of the Rhodesias and Nyasaland were much canvassed, even though any such scheme was likely to increase settler control of the overwhelmingly 'native' territories north of the Zambesi. This question was the subject of yet another monumental and inconclusive Royal Commission Report in 1939.[8]

While the vociferous political demands of the settlers tended to command the centre of the stage, the British administrators were perfecting the theory and practice of 'indirect rule'. They believed that responsibility for the African populations of the territories of East and West Africa would remain theirs indefinitely. The system was extended from areas where strong tribal authorities already existed (as in Northern Nigeria and Uganda) to territories such as Tanganyika where it was necessary to invent them. Indeed it was in Tanganyika under Lugard's disciple, Sir Donald Cameron, that the keenest exponents of the doctrine were to be found. Within this framework, the Colonial Service district officer was left with the congenial task of shepherding his charges ever so slowly along the road of political and social progress.

Indirect rule, however, was seen, in Cameron's words, as 'a bulwark against political agitation and social chaos'.[9] The emphasis on separate development within a tribal framework was anathema to the detribalised 'black European' of the west coast, living in the cities of Accra and Lagos, and certainly reflected the prejudice of the administrators against the 'educated native'. The latter, for his part, felt that the British were barring the way to political progress offered by experience of modern representative institutions and by training in modern administrative methods. Such an African wanted admission to the Civil Service as something more than a clerk, and also representation on the Legislative Council.

Even Lugard could not impose indirect rule on Southern Nigeria, and in 1922, three years after his departure, a Legislative Council was set up of forty-six members, four of the ten African representatives being elected. However, the universal acceptance of the dogmas of indirect rule in the inter-war period was to make it extremely difficult for the British to come to terms with modern nationalist movements after the Second World War.

As far as the 'development' of the African territories in an economic sense was concerned, this was generally left to private European initiative in the dependencies of central and eastern Africa. Territories were expected by the British Treasury to pay their own way, and were only allowed grants-in-aid to meet essential administrative expenditure. This meant that poor territories like British Somaliland or Northern Rhodesia before the copper boom were run on little more than a 'care and maintenance' basis, particularly when the stringent economies induced by the depression in 1931 resulted in further cuts in administrative services. The much-vaunted principle of trusteeship did not appear to involve many positive steps to promote the welfare of those on behalf of whom the trust was ostensibly exercised.

There were, however, exceptions to this rather gloomy picture. In the West African colony of the Gold Coast, an energetic governor, Sir Gordon Guggisberg, produced a ten-year plan involving the expenditure of £25 million over the period 1919–28 on roads, harbours and railways. The plan was dependent on the colony's own financial resources and could not be sustained when trading revenues fell. However, railways and roads were completed, and a deep-water harbour built at Takoradi.[10]

Apart from such examples of individual initiative based on the buoyancy of local revenues, there were indications too that, despite the dead hand of the Treasury, opinion in Whitehall was turning towards a more positive approach to colonial development. Milner and Amery, in the Chamberlain tradition, were staunch advocates in the 1920s of investment in the 'underdeveloped estates' of the Empire. In the difficult post-war world these territories were now seen as having a vital role in Britain's economic recovery. As the Colonial Secretary, L. S. Amery, put it:

> Our whole future prosperity depends not upon the uncertain prospects of European recovery, but on the development of our own heritage in the Empire.[11]

As well as the promotion of emigation to and trade with the white Dominions, Amery therefore sought to have imperial government funds made available to assist tropical colonies in development policies. But Amery was able to make little progress during the 1920s. It fell to the second Labour government to procure the enactment of the Colonial Development Act, 1929, which for the first time provided regular funds for this purpose. However, the sums involved (£1 million per annum) were too modest to have much impact, and the measure appears to have been rushed through Parliament with the object of reducing unemployment in the United Kingdom by generating orders for British manufactures from colonial governments.

It was not until the late 1930s, as Britain and the Empire slowly recovered from the effects of the Depression, that a real commitment to improving conditions in the colonial territories emerged. Whitehall was shaken by evidence of social unrest – strikes in the West Indian colonies and serious riots on the Northern Rhodesia copper belt in 1935. The lesson was brought home by the findings of a series of commissions of enquiry into conditions in the African and West Indian colonies. The Moyne Commission found in the West Indies that there was a pressing need for large expenditure on social services and development, which not even the least poor of the West Indian colonies could hope to finance from their own resources. The Commission also brought to light appalling economic and social conditions which appeared to be fairly typical of the colonial territories in general.[12] Development planning now became the order of the day in the secretariats of progressive colonial governors. The Colonial Development and Welfare Act of 1940, enacted in the darkest days of the Second World War, provided a comprehensive framework for a new policy of aid to the colonies.

The most spectacular example of 'development' – certainly in British Africa – during this period did not depend on government aid, and was financed from private British, South African and American sources. In the almost empty bush of Northern Rhodesia there developed, in the 1920s, some of the most productive copper mines in the world; by 1935 the mines were producing 146,000 tons of this vital strategic metal annually. A tropical dependency, apparently destined to be nothing but a liability when taken over from the British South Africa Company in 1924, was making a major contribution to imperial mineral resources with great financial benefit to British industry and British exports.

Nothing better illustrates the value of Chamberlain's 'undeveloped estates'.

However, for the territory concerned, the benefits were less tangible. Apart from the (low) wages paid to African miners, very little of the copper revenues went to the provision of social services or conferred economic benefits upon the African people of the territory. Traditional colonial administrative methods, moreover, were ill-suited to deal with the social problems of industrialisation; there were serious disturbances on the copperbelt in 1935 and 1940, and a total of nineteen Africans were killed by troops and police.

## The West Indies and Ceylon

Outside the huge, and generally recent, territorial acquisitions in Africa, older pieces of Empire slumbered through the inter-war years. In Malaya, for example, there were the Federated Malay States (so beloved of the popular author Somerset Maugham). These states remained under the nominal sovereignty of their native rulers who were, however, bound by treaty to act on the advice of British officials. This system came from the Indian precedent and was far older than Lugard's experiments with 'indirect rule' in Africa.

Cyprus and Malta were rather anomalous; crown colonies, inhabited by Europeans, they were sometimes restive under British rule. Malta seemed too small and too vital for imperial defence to allow progression to Dominion status. Cyprus was divided by the hostility of the Greek and Turkish communities, and in 1931 experienced anti-government disturbances.

In the West Indies, the economic and social problems analysed by the 1938 Moyne Commission were exacerbated by racial tension and discrimination. Whereas in East Africa there were well-defined conflicts of interests between the three racial groups (native African and immigrant Indian and European) in the West Indies the problem was infinitely more complex: the African, European, Indian and Chinese groups were all 'immigrants', and the Europeans had been established since the seventeenth century. The gradations of colour in a society where most people were of 'mixed' race also reflected social and economic position, with the blackest people at the bottom of the pile.

However, unlike the negroes of Africa, the West Indian negroes, the descendants of slaves brought from Africa to work the sugar plantations, shared the language, religion and culture of the whites – thus exposing more starkly the discriminatory nature of the islands' society. For the exceptionally gifted dark-skinned boy – reared on a strange diet of cricket and the English classics –there was a very narrow gate through which he might pass to education, professional status, wealth and even a seat on the local Legislative Council. Some few passed to even greater fame as cricketers. The most famous of West Indian cricketers of this period, Learie Constantine, came to England to play in the Lancashire League, became a local hero there, and awakened in ordinary Englishmen as no professional politician or publicist could have done, an interest in the millions of non-white citizens of the Empire.[13]

Such exceptional cases, however, only served to emphasise the dominance by whites and near-whites of the business and political life of West Indian island society. Black West Indians intensely resented being equated with uncivilised or half-civilised 'natives' in other parts of the colonial Empire, and demanded 'the British right to govern ourselves'. However, the oligarchical nature of West Indian political society appeared to bar the way to responsible government. In Jamaica, for example, politically the most advanced community, less than one-twelfth of the population qualified for the vote in 1936.

The slow constitutional progress of increasing the elected element in local legislatures was hardly relevant to the aspirations of the black working class. The economic distress of the 1930s produced widespread strikes and disorder in many of the islands between 1934 and 1938, during which some fifty people were killed. The disturbances led to widespread publicity being given in London to conditions in the West Indies (which had previously attracted little attention, except of course in cricketing circles!) and to the appointment of the 1938 Moyne Royal Commission, a body of unusual size and brilliance. The Commission's recommendations paved the way for substantial political advance during the Second World War, and by 1944 Jamaica had achieved 'semi-responsible' government. Moreover, the black working class in the larger islands had found an effective voice in organised labour under the leadership of such colourful figures as Alexander Bustamente, destined in 1962 to become the first premier of an independent Jamaica. In the West Indies immediately before the Second World War it is thus possible to see the beginning of the new black

Commonwealth which is conventionally regarded as being heralded by the Watson Report on the Gold Coast in 1948. The larger West Indian islands had started hesitantly on the path to full self-government within the Commonwealth.

Much more remarkable was the inter-war constitutional progress of Ceylon, the great dependency whose governorship was traditionally the most sought-after prize in the Colonial Service. Here it was established clearly that progress to responsible government was within the grasp of non-white portions of the Empire when the achievement of that goal even by India remained (publicly at least) in the indefinite future. The turning point for Ceylon was the Donoughmore Report on the constitution in 1928.[14] The report did not recommend an immediate grant of responsible government since, as only 4 per cent of the population had the vote under the existing system, this would be tantamount to placing a small and wealthy oligarchy in power. (Strangely no such inhibition had prevented the transfer of power in Southern Rhodesia in 1923 to an equally small minority of Europeans.) The Donoughmore Report recommended, however, the immediate concession of the vote to all men over twenty-one and all women over thirty, the franchise reached in Great Britain itself only ten years before.

Democracy had thus come to the non-white Commonwealth. The report also led to the introduction of a highly complex system of semi-responsible government which meant that in respect of certain 'transferred subjects' Ceylonese ministers were responsible to the popularly elected legislature. British-style parliamentary institutions were thus given an opportunity to take root in Ceylon before independence – something to prove rare in the non-white Commonwealth.


## INDIA, 1919–39: THE ROAD TO *SWARAJ*

India remained the centrepiece of the imperial structure. Even in 1939 few men in British public life would have dissented from the view of Lord Curzon, expressed in 1901, that the loss of India would mean that Britain would 'drop straightaway to a third-rate power'. By 1939, however, it was difficult to believe in the feasibility of maintaining British 'rule' in the form of the old self-confident benevolent imperialism epitomised by Curzon's Viceroyalty.

The problem between the wars appeared to be the need to satisty Indian national aspirations by the concession of self-government while retaining India as a part of the imperial system. In place of Curzon's unquestioning acceptance of Britain's right and duty to rule India's millions, Lord Irwin (Edward Wood, later Lord Halifax, Viceroy 1926–31), of gaunt and sombre mien, now personified the anguish of a declining imperial power faced with the loss of her 'brightest jewel'. British prestige in the East was gone, he told a packed and incredulous meeting of Conservative MPs on his return from India (though he rather surprisingly attributed this collapse to the Russo-Japanese war and the looseness of western women as depicted in films).[15]

The concern of Irwin's audience reflected the priorities of Conservative MPs who, with a few exceptions such as Harold Macmillan, were far more concerned about India in the early 1930s than they were about unemployment. India was then 'perhaps the central issue in parliamentary life'.[16] Its problems apparently imbued even the phlegmatic Conservative leader Stanley Baldwin with a Gladstonian sense of mission and almost wrecked the political career of Winston Churchill when he resigned the Tory whip over Indian advance. At one point it appeared that the whole fate of the Empire was bound up with the issue of Indian constitutional progress.

The Montagu–Chelmsford reforms had introduced some elements of local responsibility into the provincial governments of British India, but at the centre the government of India remained essentially autocratic despite the provision for the appointment of more Indian members of the Viceroy's Council. Even the appointment of an Indian Viceroy, however, would not have affected the constitutional subordination of the government of India to Whitehall.

In recognition of India's wartime services to the Empire, and of her right to eventual self-government, Indian representatives were admitted to the Imperial War Cabinet and War Conferences of 1917. India was also a signatory of the Treaty of Versailles, and, although not 'fully self-governing' as required by the Covenant, became a member of the League of Nations. However, this fine show was without real substance. The reality was exposed in 1922 when Edwin Montagu, Secretary of State for India, in his capacity as spokesman for the government of India, published criticisms of the proposed peace treaty with Turkey. Montagu was forced to resign: like any other British minister, the Indian Secretary was bound by the principle of Cabinet solidarity.

So long as there was no devolution of political responsibility at the centre, such concessions as the acceptance in 1921 of the principle of fiscal autonomy for India could not satisfy Indian nationalist aspirations – particularly in the light of developments in other parts of the Empire in the years following the First World War. The Anglo-Irish treaty of 1921, the formal recognition of Egyptian independence in 1922, even evidence of constitutional progress in neighbouring Ceylon, all seemed to throw into relief India's continuing subordination.

In Indian eyes there was a serious drawback even to the ultimate goal of responsible government within the Empire pledged by Montagu in 1917. Full membership of the Commonwealth of Nations was at present confined to countries where political power was exclusively in European hands. This was true even in South Africa with its large non-white majority that included a substantial number of Indians. Before the First World War, Mahatma Gandhi, who was to play such a fateful part in the independence struggle in India, had organised the *satyagraha* or passive resistance movement against the discrimination practised against those of Indian origin in the Union. At the Imperial Conference of 1921 the Indian representatives sponsored a resolution recognising:

> the incongruity between the position of India as an equal member of the British Empire and the existence of disabilities upon British Indians lawfully domiciled in some other parts of the Empire.[17]

As Srinivasa Sastri, a leading Indian 'moderate', told the Conference: 'This is a resolution that will be regarded in India as the test by which the whole position must be judged'.

Gandhi, who after his return to India had entered national politics in 1919, symbolised the link between the struggle for equality of treatment of Indians in other parts of the Empire with the movement for national independence at home. In both spheres, Indians had reason to doubt the Empire's good intentions on the issue of race equality. Abroad, the discriminatory policies of the South African government were intensified, and Indians were denied equal political rights with white settlers in the British colony of Kenya, while in another British colony, Southern Rhodesia, responsible government was conceded in 1923 to a tiny European minority with an electorate of 18,000.

At home, the aftermath of the 1919 Amritsar massacre was more damaging to Anglo-Indian relations than the deed itself; support for this display of 'firmness', both among the British community in India and in the Imperial Parliament, shocked Indian opinion and convinced many of the realities of British racial arrogance and of the fundamentally oppressive nature of British rule. Gandhi, who had stood for co-operation in the implementation of the Montagu–Chelmsford reforms, now proclaimed that 'co-operation in any shape or form with this satanic government is sinful'.

By and large, however, the Indian government was able to cope with the *satyagraha* tactics which Gandhi adapted from his South Africa days. Gandhi's appeal to the masses converted Congress from an upper-middle-class pressure group into a truly popular movement, yet, though committed to substantial social change, he was not a political revolutionary. In this sense Gandhi served the government of India's purpose by inhibiting an outright Congress commitment to the achievement of *Swaraj*, or 'self-rule', by revolutionary violence. Instead Gandhi believed that 'the Englishman is very mortally afraid of his own conscience if you ever appeal to it and show him to be in the wrong'.

In dealing with Gandhi's campaigns, however, the government was able to avoid any repetition of the terrible events that shook the Punjab in 1919 and which might have proved unacceptable at home as a basis for maintaining British control in India. Gandhi, of course, was locked up from time to time, but a framework for collaboration remained. If Gandhi was rather naïve in his approach to the British, he and the rest of the Congress leadership seriously underestimated the communal problem. Just as the British in their turn were reluctant to believe that the Congress 'extremists' enjoyed real popular support, so neither the apolitical idealist Gandhi nor the secular socialist Jawaharlal Nehru (subsequently Indian Prime Minister 1947–64) gave sufficient weight to Muslim fears that Congress stood for the replacement of the British Raj by a Hindu Raj.

Against this complex background, the 1919 dyarchy scheme (or rule by both races) came into operation in 1921, The majority of Congress opposed 'Council-entry', as it was termed; a minority formed the *Swaraj* party and sought election to the legislatures; some even accepted ministerial office in the provincial governments. In the central legislature, a *Swarajist* majority tried, for a time, a policy of obstruction. This did no more than embarrass the government, which was not responsible to that legislature. Lord Birkenhead, Secretary of State for India, was determined for his part that no steps towards responsible government at the centre should be made. To him it was 'frankly inconceivable that India would ever be fit for Dominion self-government'.

In order to pre-empt action by a possible future Labour government in Britain, Birkenhead brought forward the appointment of a Statutory Commission to investigate the working of the 1919 Act. The Commission, under Sir John Simon, began work in 1928 in the face of an extensive boycott in India. In a monumental act of tactlessness the Simon Commission chose not to appoint any Indian members, and a committee under Motilal Nehru, Jawaharlal's father, produced an alternative report demanding immediate self-government within the Commonwealth.

The Simon Report was, in any case, destined to be overtaken by events. In 1929, the Conservatives were indeed replaced by a Labour minority government. The Labour leaders were believed to favour an early grant of self-government to India, and were likely to prove more responsive than their predecessors in office to the desire of Lord Irwin, the Viceroy, to make a strong and memorable gesture of friendship to the Indians and 'so to restore faith in the ultimate purpose of British policy'. This gesture took the form of the announcement in October 1929 of a 'Round Table' conference at which the Princely States and all sections of opinion in British India would be represented; this was combined with a clear statement that the natural issue of India's constitutional progress as contemplated in the declaration of 1917 was the attainment of Dominion status.[18]

The 'Irwin Declaration', which may appear to have done no more than spell out what was implicit in Montagu's statement of 1917, added fuel to the mounting political crisis in India and brought India to the centre of the political stage in London. Congress soon discovered that Britain considered that Dominion status still lay in the indefinite future. It therefore resolved to boycott the Round Table Conference, and in March 1930 Gandhi embarked on the most famous of his civil disobedience campaigns, the Dandi Salt March. To the more radical Congressmen, including the younger Nehru, even Dominion status smacked of inferiority and no longer satisfied their concept of *Swaraj*.

Indian suspicions of British intentions (suspicions which Irwin had hoped to allay) were further enhanced by the explosion of anger and indignation provoked on the Conservative and Liberal benches in the Imperial Parliament by the explicit reference to Dominion status in relation to India. It was appreciated that in the light of the Balfour Definition of 1926 this was tantamount to the promise of full independence. Even those Conservatives who had come to accept the inevitability of progressive steps towards Indian self-government were 'astonished and almost horrified'. The Tory 'diehards', led rather incongruously by Winston Churchill (who had been a member of the government responsible for the Morley–Minto Reforms and negotiator of the Anglo-Irish Treaty in 1921) envisaged the repetition of the process whereby Southern Ireland had been effectively lost to the Empire. The diehards, therefore, were opposed bitterly to any measures which might appear as concessions brought about by Congress agitation; concessions thus made out of 'weakness', and symptomatic of the defeatism which was corroding the Raj. To Churchill, Irwin's policy was indicative of national decline: 'We are suffering from a disease of the will. We are the victims of nervous collapse, of a morbid state of mind'.[19]

Churchill warned that loss of confidence in Britain's mission in the East would strip her presence there of every moral sanction. The debate on India thus raised issues which were central to the survival of the British imperial system. For if Britain were to lose the 'moral authority' to govern her vast Empire, then surely the days of that Empire were numbered? Certainly those responsible for the administration of Empire understood the moral factor which might also be called bluff. Thus General Dyer at Amritsar carefully calculated the amount of firing required to produce 'a sufficient moral effect from the military point of view . . . throughout the Punjab'.

In the face of the Civil Disobedience campaign of 1930, the Home Member of the Viceroy's Council privately expressed his concern that: 'Government may not be retaining that essential moral superiority which is perhaps the most important factor in this struggle'.[20] In general political terms these anxieties, most eloquently voiced by Churchill, found expression in the view that any constitutional concessions in India should be made only after a prolonged display of firmness had re-established the moral authority of the Imperial Government in the face of Congress agitation.

The view which prevailed among both Labour ministers and the Conservative leadership in the National Government that had replaced Labour in 1931 accepted that Indian government should be based on the assent of the governed. The alternative, said Wedgwood Benn, the Labour India Secretary, was government by force, which he condemned both on practical and on moral grounds. The Conservative leader, Stanley Baldwin, spoke in terms which were to be echoed by Harold Macmillan in Cape Town a quarter of a century later:

> We have taught [India] the lesson [of democracy] and she wants us to pay the bill. There is a wind of nationalism and freedom blowing round the world and blowing as strongly in Asia as anywhere else in the world.[21]

The British were still able to ensure, however, that the pace of Indian constitutional advance should be determined by themselves with appropriate consultation of Indian opinion. The massive Government of India Act 1935, the longest Act on the British statute book, had its eventual painful birth out of three Round Table Conferences between 1930–2, the White Paper of 1933, and the Joint Select Committee of 1933–4, culminating in Parliamentary debates containing nearly 2000 speeches and totalling $15\frac{1}{2}$ million words.

The scheme which thus emerged was of appalling complexity in an attempt to secure the co-operation of the Indian Princes, sufficient recognition of the communal principle to satisfy the Muslims and other minorities, concessions to popular government to appease nationalist sentiment, and the 'safeguards' considered essential by the imperial power. Briefly, the 1935 Act provided that dyarchy should be replaced by responsible government in the provinces, but should reappear at the centre, where a federal executive would be created consisting of popularly responsible ministers controlling the whole administration except defence and foreign affairs, which would remain in the hands of the Viceroy's nominees. The central portion of the scheme was destined never to come into operation. It depended on the agreement of rulers representing half the princely population, and this had not been secured at the outbreak of the Second World War. Even this unrealised 'Federation of India', however, would not have enjoyed

Dominion status for the 1935 constitution retained the elements of legislative and executive subordination to London.

The Act pleased neither the diehards in London (Churchill called it a monstrous monument of shame built by pigmies) nor the Congress in India. R. A. Butler, then Indian Under-Secretary, subsequently considered that the need to overcome Conservative opposition at home distracted ministers from an effort to draw closer to the Congress movement and to confront the realities of Indian politics. The great gulf between the British and Congress was most nearly bridged in 1931 by Gandhi, who was the Congress leader most favourably disposed to co-operation with the British, and Irwin, a deeply religious man who appeared an ideal subject for Gandhi's appeal to conscience.

The Gandhi–Irwin Pact, however, and Gandhi's participation in the second Round Table conference did not break the deadlock on the issue of immediate independence. Apparently Irwin himself had hoped to build a breakwater against future trouble by dividing Gandhi and the more conservative politicians in India from the younger Nehru and the more extreme nationalists. In the event, civil disobedience was resumed in 1932 but was firmly and successfully dealt with by Irwin's successor, Lord Willingdon (Viceroy 1931–6). This firmness was well received in London, and not only by the Tory diehards. As Butler noted, 'there was always a cheer when the House [of Commons] learnt that people had been locked up or firm action had been taken'.[22] There had indeed been widespread anxiety about the loss of face involved in Irwin's dealings with Gandhi, an anxiety most violently expressed by Churchill who confessed himself alarmed and nauseated by the spectacle of Gandhi:

> a seditious Middle Temple lawyer, now posing as a fakir of a type well-known in the East, striding half-naked up the steps of the Viceregal Palace . . . there to negotiate and to parley on equal terms with the Representative of the King-Emperor.[23]

Such words were not to be easily forgiven in India, nor, indeed, in Britain.

The first provincial elections under the 1935 Act were held in 1937. The extent of the Congress victories – absolute majorities in six of the eleven provinces in British India, and the largest single party in three more – appeared to confound those in the government of India who clung to the belief that Congress did not represent the views of the Indian people as a whole. But these victories confirmed also the fears of those who saw the new constitutional arrangements as a springboard for Congress to capture power.

The poor showing of the Muslim League also cast doubt on the strenth of communalism as a political force. To Nehru, who had masterminded the Congress campaign, a victory had been won over the combined forces of imperialism, feudalism and communalism. However, as Congress ministries took power, at least at provincial level, they were faced with the problems of responsibility, of delivering some of the promises made to the Indian masses. It was no longer a question of co-operation or non-co-operation with the Raj, in most matters affecting the daily lives of the population at large in several provinces Congress *was* the Raj.

The strains were already beginning to tell when the Congress ministries resigned after the outbreak of the Second World War in 1939. There was another ominous portent. Confident in their electoral triumph of 1937, Congress had declined to share power with the Muslim League. The League leader, Mohamed Ali Jinnah, then worked furiously to rally all Muslims to his communal banner. By the outbreak of war he had in large measure succeeded, and the Muslims celebrated the departure of the Congress ministers as 'Deliverance Day' – deliverance from the tyranny, oppression and injustice of the Congress Raj in the provinces. The road to partition lay ahead.

By 1939 the rapid achievement of Indian independence had become a certainty which even the crisis of the Second World War could not affect in the long run, though it involved renewed bitter clashes between Congress and the British. Britain had not had her hold on her Indian Empire broken simply by Congress agitation; in that sense the government of India had won nearly all the battles. However, the drive towards independence had now acquired a momentum which few in Britain had the will or desire to resist, certainly not by the forcible suppression of the national movement. As Professor Low has written:

there can be very little doubt that by the time of the Second World War the great debate on India, in Britain at least, was over.[24]

He then quotes from a letter written by a London journalist in 1940:

The diehards are extinct, public opinion is united in desiring India to obtain her independence just as soon as it can be arranged.

## INTER-IMPERIAL RELATIONS: THE BALFOUR DEFINITION AND BEYOND

*The Constitutional Settlement: The Balfour Definition and the Statute of Westminster*

1914–18 imperial organisation soon went the way of the rest of the Lloyd George system. The Imperial War Cabinet lingered on into 1919 under the guise of the British Empire Delegation to the Peace Conferences. Eventually, however, the Dominion ministers went home to face pressing domestic problems, and in Britain Lloyd George rather reluctantly reverted to the old, peacetime Cabinet.

The next imperial gathering, in 1921, turned out not to be Lloyd George's vision of an 'Imperial Peace Cabinet' but a conference of prime ministers on the pre-war model. Lloyd George's rhetoric survived – 'today', he proclaimed, 'the Empire is in charge of Downing Street' – but zeal for imperial constitutional engineering had not. The 1917 plan for a post-war constitutional conference was abandoned. In the view of the Australian premier, 'Billy' Hughes, such a conference could do only mischief since the Dominions already had 'all the rights of self-government enjoyed by independent nations'. General Smuts, who had recently fought two general elections in South Africa on the issue of secession, sought to meet Opposition criticism in South Africa and crystallise his own vision of the Commonwealth by persuading Britain and the Dominions to adopt a 'declaration of constitutional right'. For the time being, Hughes' view prevailed. 'The constitutional tinkers', he cabled exultantly back to Australia, 'are securely soldered up in their own can'.[25]

The next conference, in 1923, was dominated by foreign and economic affairs (see below), but in 1926 the constitutional issue was revived. There was now more general support for the elimination of the formal elements of subordination in the relationship between Britain and the Dominions. General Hertzog, Smuts' successor as prime minister in 1924, and political rival, came armed ironically with Smuts' own proposal for a declaration of political right; at the same time Canada's Liberal isolationist premier William Lyon Mackenzie King was smarting from a brush with his Governor-General Lord Byng over the exercise of the royal prerogative in refusing a dissolution of parliament. Moreover, there was now a cuckoo on the imperial nest in the form of the Irish Free State, the newest and most reluctant Dominion. In southern Ireland, as in South Africa, Republican sentiment was strong, and having wrung the reluctant concession of Dominion status out of Lloyd George in 1921, the Irish wished to ensure that status was equated with sovereign independence.

There was, perhaps surprisingly, no reluctance on the British side to satisfy Dominion aspirations. Unionist ex-premier Lord Balfour, who chaired the conference's Inter-imperial Relations Committee, and Leopold Amery, first holder of the new office of Secretary of State for Dominion affairs, both played a constructive part in the conference. If Australia and New Zealand were still suspicious of constitutional 'tinkering' they could hardly be *plus royaliste que le roi*, so all of this meant that the discussions were conducted in an atmosphere of good feeling and mutual accommodation.

The report of the Inter-imperial Relation Committee embodied the famous 'Balfour definition', clarifying the position and mutual relation of Great Britain and the Dominions in terms of equality of status:

> They are autonomous communities within the British Empire, equal in status, in no way subordinate one to another in any aspect of their domestic or external affairs, though united by a common allegiance to the Crown, and freely associated as members of the British Commonwealth of Nations.[26]

This delicately balanced compromise reflected the existing situation, not a constitutional advance. Its references to common allegiance to the Crown and free association satisfied those who were concerned about the preservation of Commonwealth unity, while the emphasis on Dominion autonomy and non-subordination satisfied Hertzog's desire to slay the dragon of the Empire-superstate and procure recognition of South Africa's independence. 'I have no fear of Empire any longer', he declared on his return to Cape Town.[27]

The 1926 Inter-imperial Relations Committee also considered

specific areas where the constitutional position was (at least formally) inconsistent with the 'equality of status' principle. For example, the Committee's recommendation that the Governor-General of a Dominion should cease to be the formal channel of communication between the British government and the government of that Dominion, led to the appointment of British High Commissioners in Dominion capitals to perform quasi-diplomatic functions; the first such appointment was that of Sir William Clark to Ottawa in 1928.

In addition, the complexity of the issues involved in the operation of Dominion legislation, and the operation of legislation passed by the 'Imperial' parliament at Westminster in relation to the Dominions, necessitated the convening of a special conference of experts in 1929. Its recommendations were embodied in the famous Statute of Westminster enacted in 1931, after being approved by the Imperial Conference of 1930. The Statute stipulated that henceforth the Parliament of the United Kingdom should not legislate for a Dominion except by the consent of that Dominion (this had, in fact, long been the conventional position), and that no law made by the Parliament of a Dominion should be invalidated on grounds of repugnancy to English law. Thus the Dominion Parliaments achieved equality of status with Westminster, and no longer could they be regarded, even formally, as subordinate legislatures of an 'Imperial Parliament'. This was not a mere technicality; in 1926, the Judicial Committee of the Privy Council had declared a section of the Canadian Criminal Code to be 'void and inoperative' in so far as it was repugnant to earlier 'Imperial' legislation.

These matters were non-controversial in the sense that the United Kingdom government, which had been one of the authors of the Balfour definition, did not seek to resist the removal of such formal elements of subordination. But the discussion of law and constitutional theory at the Imperial Conferences of 1929 and 1930 could be used by some of the delegations, particularly the Irish and South Africans, for the furthering of national political goals. If the dismantling of much of the legal and symbolic structure of the Commonwealth was welcome to the Irish and South Africans, and to a lesser extent in Canada, by 1931 it was regarded with misgiving in New Zealand and Australia, and by some conservative elements in Britain. 'We have torn down a castle to build a row of villas' was the trenchant observation of the Australian R. G. Casey, later to be his country's Governor-General. Winston Churchill, faced with the reduction of generous sentiments into the language of acts of Parliament, saw the clauses of the Statute of Westminster as 'pedantic, painful, and, to some at any rate, almost repellent'.[28]

## Foreign Affairs, Defence and Trade

In one respect, the story of this period closely reflects the constitutional developments recounted in the last section. 'Equality of Status' was given a further dimension by the emergence of the Dominions as individual sovereign members of the community of nations; for the first time the Empire ceased to be one diplomatic unity.

Of wider historical significance, however, is the extent to which the evolving Commonwealth relationship affected the position of the partner states in the face of the crises of the inter-war period – in particular the economic depression of the early 1930s and the growing threat to security presented by the Italian, Japanese and German dictatorships.

Here equality of status could not possibly mean equality of function. By virtue of her relatively enormous political and economic power and responsibilities, Britian was inevitably entitled to a dominant position in imperial counsels; she had vast areas of concern and responsibility in Europe and the dependent Empire which scarcely concerned the Dominions.

Where particular Dominion interests were involved, a sense of common purpose was not always easy to achieve. In some areas, such as disarmament, the Empire/Commonwealth was able to maintain a common policy with relative ease. But the 1920s soon showed that the pre-war dream of a truly 'imperial' foreign policy, in the making of which all members of the Commonwealth would participate, had to be abandoned for ever. Essentially, neither Britain nor the Dominions wished to limit their own freedom of action.

These developments may be traced through discussions of foreign policy and defence in successive Imperial Conferences. In 1921, 'Billy' Hughes, the Australian premier, still emphasised unity and the need for more effective consultative machinery:

> The Dominions and Great Britain were still one and indivisible: it was essential that British foreign policy should be moulded by the Empire as a whole and not by Great Britain alone.[29]

For such a common policy to be implemented, however, an elaborate bureaucratic machine, agreement on common objectives and a willingness to share commitment and responsibility were necessary. These ingredients were soon proved lacking. Even the 1921 Imperial Conference, where agreement was reached on a common Empire position on Pacific questions in preparation for the coming conference in Washington with the United States, Japan and France, revealed important differences. Hughes clashed violently with Arthur Meighan, the Canadian Prime Minister, over the renewal of the Anglo-Japanese alliance. The Australians wished to retain it as a gurantee of their security, whereas the Canadians, secure in their North American 'fire-proof house' wished to abandon the treaty in order to appease the United States. Nevertheless the British Empire did function smoothly as a diplomatic unit on the Versailles precedent at the Washington Conference, 1921–2. This eventually produced a vaguely worded pact between the US, the British Empire, Japan and France, which was considered to replace the Anglo-Japanese alliance: a treaty on limitation of naval armaments settled a 5 : 5 : 3 ratio between the British Empire, the US and Japan.

The fundamental problems, however, still remained: other than for a 'set-piece' such as Washington there was no effective machinery for evolving and executing a common policy; nor were the Dominions prepared to accept an equitable share of the peacetime defence burden. With the British navy apparently supreme and with much talk of disarmament, it was hardly surprising that only Australia and New Zealand showed much enthusiasm for the Admiralty's proposed new naval base at Singapore, or that Lord Jellicoe's plan for a powerful British Commonwealth Far Eastern Fleet was stillborn.

Much emphasis has been laid on the importance of the Chanak incident in 1922 as an indication of the centrifugal tendencies in the post-war Empire. Certainly an impulsive and inept appeal by Lloyd George and Churchill for Dominion help in a British confrontation with Turkey in Asia Minor revealed that the Dominions could no longer be relied upon to give automatic military support to Britain in any quarrel. While Australia and New Zealand were prepared to respond at once, the Canadian Prime Minister, Mackenzie King, replied that Canadian participation would depend on the decision of the Canadian Parliament.

No doubt the consequences of this Lloyd George–Churchill

*gaffe* – as much regarded as an aberration in Whitehall as in the Dominions – could have been minimised had there existed a firm resolve on all sides to improve the machinery of co-operation. However, governments both in Britain and in the Dominions – whose number had recently been augmented by a reluctant Irish Free State – were not prepared to sacrifice their own freedom of action for the sake of closer imperial links. This trend became clear at the 1923 Conference, the published summary of which was at pains to emphasise the non-executive character of the gathering:

> This conference is a conference of representatives of the several governments of the Empire; its views and conclusions on foreign policy are necessarily subject to the action of the Governments and Parliaments of the various portions of the Empire . . . .[30]

The British official papers now available to historians make it clear that Britain had abandoned any attempt to restrict Dominion freedom of action. Thus Mackenzie King found that the ground over which he expected to fight was conceded readily. In this atmosphere, Dominion autonomy made great strides. While lip-service continued to be paid to the diplomatic unity of the Empire, the right of the Dominions to separate diplomatic representation in foreign capitals and to independence in the treaty-making sphere was recognised. For their part, the British government were free to deal with European problems without Dominion involvement. Thus Lord Curzon, the British Foreign Secretary, was able to negotiate alone a new settlement of the Turkish problem finalised in the Treaty of Lausanne in 1923.

The Treaty of Locarno of 1925, which involved British guarantees of the French and German frontiers, expressly provided that neither the Dominions nor India should be bound without their consent. India's exclusion, however, was essentially anomalous since, in the last resort, the Indian government was subject to the absolute control of the British government in such matters. No attempt was made to involve the Dominions in these negotiations, which the Canadian Minister of Justice, Lapointe, called a 'European matter', and none of the Dominions did in fact assume obligations under Locarno.

Of course co-operation continued to be close between the British and Dominion delegations at international conferences involving matters of common concern. On a day-to-day basis the Dominions also continued to rely heavily on information channelled from the British Foreign Office through the new 'Dominions Office' established in 1925. Dominion diplomatic representation remained miniscule in comparision with that of Great Britain which continued to act as 'managing agent' in relation to multitudinous imperial diplomatic tasks.

The Empire had, however, ceased to be a diplomatic unit. As S. M. Bruce of Australia suggested in 1926, the new Commonwealth was 'governed by an unwritten treaty of mutual guarantee'. This meant, for example, that Britain would normally expect to be assured of Dominion support in any future major crisis. But it did not mean that such support would be automatically forthcoming. According to the Nationalist Prime Minister of South Africa, General Hertzog, the logic of the freedom of action in foreign relations conceded to the Dominions was that each individual Dominion had the right to remain neutral in any conflict between Great Britain and another state.

Against this background, the strengths and weaknesses of the Commonwealth system of co-operation, as evolved in the hopeful atmosphere of the 1920s, were to be tested during the economic crisis of 1931 and subsequently amid the growing threat presented by the Italian, German and Japanese dictatorships, a threat that was to lead to the involvement of the whole Commonwealth (except the Irish Free State) in the Second World War. How did the now fully self-governing Commonwealth respond to the economic and political crises of the 1930s?

Since Joseph Chamberlain's day, advocates of some form of imperial preference had seen both political and economic advantages in such a scheme. The issue was closely linked to British domestic politics, since progress towards such a system would only be possible if Great Britain were completely to abandon free trade, still regarded by many as sacred. Despite the emergency introduction of some protective duties during the First World War, the Conservative defeat at the 1923 general election suggested that protection had retained its pre-war unpopularity with the British voter. Stanley Baldwin, the Conservative Prime Minister, had gone to the country on a protectionist platform, certainly encouraged by the strong sentiments expressed in favour of imperial preference at the Imperial Economic Conference held shortly before the election. His defeat resulted in the formation of the first Labour government. However, after the 1929 election had shown that the Conservatives could be beaten even with their free trade colours nailed to the mast, a new crusade for 'Empire Free Trade' (a nice example of Orwellian doublespeak) was launched, backed by the press lords Northcliffe and Rothermere. It was that campaign which caused Baldwin, whose position as Conservative leader was endangered, to denounce Rothermere as wanting 'power without responsibility, the prerogative of the harlot throughout the ages'.

The onset of the world economic depression at the end of 1929, causing unemployment to rise steeply throughout the Commonwealth, made politicians desperate for any possible allevi-ation of economic distress. In the 1930 Canadian general election the Conservative R. B. Bennett, a friend of his fellow Canadian Lord Beaverbrook, defeated Mackenzie King on a platform of imperial preference, and went on to press his case strongly at the Imperial Conference of 1930. But he met strong resistance to any change in British fiscal policies from the Chancellor of the Exchequer in the British Labour government, Philip Snowden (who as early as 1903 had challenged Chamberlain's tariff reform programme), and who clung to free trade with Gladstonian zeal. However, Bennett was successful in his plea for a further Imperial Economic Conference which met in Ottawa under his chairman-ship in 1932.

By this time the Labour governmmnt in Britain had been replaced by a National government, and Neville Chamberlain, a protectionist like his father, had replaced Snowden as Chancellor of the Exchequer. After much hard bargaining the Conference produced the so-called 'Ottawa Agreements', a series of bilateral arrangements for mutual tariff concessions between various Com-monwealth countries. These hardly amounted to a realisation of the dream of those who saw a greater degree of Empire economic unity as an alternative to the now vanished hopes of political unity.

The early 1930s, however, were not a time of vision, and each set of Commonwealth ministers was absorbed in the problems of its own country. Snowden resigned from the National government as a result of Ottawa, complaining that the British delegation had returned 'after weeks of acrimonious disputes and sordid struggles with vested interests, with agreements wrenched from them to avert a collapse, and an exposure to the world of the hollowness of the talk of Imperial sentiment in economic affairs'.[31] Inter-imperial trade, however, did increase: for example, between 1931 and 1937, UK imports from the Dominions, India and the Colonies increased from

24 per cent of total overseas trade to 37 per cent; and exports from 32 per cent to 39 per cent. Another important economic link was provided by the sterling 'bloc' or 'sterling area' as it later became known. This had originated as an act of self-preservation when Britain and other countries were forced off the gold standard by the economic blizzard of 1931. The 'bloc' consisted of the whole Commonwealth (minus Canada) plus some small foreign countries, and basically meant that the pound sterling replaced gold as their monetary standard, and members operated what was in effect a common currency for foreign exchange purposes.

After the Second World War, the Ottawa system of tariff preferences and the functioning of the sterling area helped to maintain the importance of Commonwealth economic and financial links as the political element in the Commonwealth connection weakened. The post-war Commonwealth, as J. D. B. Miller has said, 'was much more of an economic unit than it had ever been before'. Even in the 1970s, attempts to revive the Commonwealth were centred in the economic sphere – for example, British Prime Minister Harold Wilson's proposals to the 1975 meeting of Commonwealth heads of government.[32]

In the sphere of international relations and defence, the 1930s saw the development of some threat to almost every part of the Empire/Commonwealth – except Canada, secure as ever in her 'fire-proof house'. Britain faced a threat from growing German and Italian aggression in Europe and the Near East; Australia and New Zealand, and even India, were threatened by the growth of Japanese power in the Far East; even South Africa was conscious of German designs for the recovery of South West Africa (administered by the Union under a League of Nations mandate since 1919), and the British mandated territory of Tanganyika. Different interests and policies, however, made effective co-operation difficult. Moreover, to some statesmen, both in Great Britain and the Dominions, the concept of collective security through the League of Nations appeared more attractive than the idea of 'imperial' defence. Thus if there were deep Canadian suspicions that the obligations contained in the League covenant would somehow entangle Canada in European conflicts, the Irish Free State saw the League as a useful counterbalance to the Commonwealth connection, a sentiment that found some echo in nationalist circles in South Africa. To the Irish and South Africans in particular, the League provided a welcome opportunity to advertise their independence in international affairs. As individual members of the League, however, the Dominions were of little international importance. Their importance lay in the extent to which they influenced the shaping of British foreign policy.

The evidence uncovered by historians from the public records suggests that this influence was relatively slight. British consultation with Dominion governments was often belated and perfunctory. For example, its inadequacy during key developments in the crisis provoked by the Italian invasion of Abyssinia in 1935 drew a bitterly censorious private protest message from the South African government, which in turn aroused considerable resentment in London. When Britain took the lead in proposing to the League the abandonment of sanctions against Italy in 1936, New Zealand supported their maintenance during the debate, and South Africa went so far as to cast the only dissenting vote against the British proposal.[33]

In the last analysis, Dominion opinion opposed to British policy was discounted in Whitehall. Where Dominion support was forthcoming, however, that support was used by British politicians to justify the policies they had already resolved upon. 'Dominion opinion' eased the British government's task in selling their policy both to public opinion and to foreign governments.

This process can be seen most clearly in relation to the policy of 'appeasement' of Germany adopted by Neville Chamberlain after he succeeded Stanley Baldwin as British Prime Minister in 1937. From a Commonwealth standpoint, the attraction was that it was perhaps the only policy which, for a variety of differing reasons, could attract general support. The British sought to satisfy German ambitions in Europe in a way which would preserve peace without sacrificing vital British interests; the Irish were intent on neutrality in any European conflict; Canadian ministers wished to avoid any obligations in Europe which would be criticised by isolationists and French separatists at home. In South Africa there was considerable pro-Nazi sentiment among Afrikaners, and at a secret meeting of Commonwealth prime ministers in 1935 during the celebrations for George V's Silver Jubilee, the South African Prime Minister, General Hertzog, had expressed sympathy for the 'injustices' suffered by Germany at Versailles. It was hardly surprising, therefore, that the South African High Commissioner in London was actively involved in discouraging any British intervention when Hitler reoccupied the Rhineland in 1936. Even Australia and New

Zealand were understandably anxious lest undue emphasis on the threat from Germany should downgrade the threat from Japan in their 'near north'. Appeasement of Germany, therefore, certainly appeared as the policy which divided the Commonwealth least.

It could, of course, be said that Dominion opinion affected British policy-making in a purely negative way. While it did not cause Neville Chamberlain to adopt the policy that he did, it would have made any more robust policy less appealing. 'The influence of the Dominions', says Keith Middlemas, 'in the two years before the outbreak of war . . . represented a major external handicap on any policy designed to strengthen *European* security against Hitler'.[34]

At the Imperial Conference in 1937 – destined to be the last gathering of its kind – discussion of imperial defence was hampered by the South African and Canadian refusal to attend meetings of the Committee of Imperial Defence. The latter ceased to perform its traditional function as a forum for British and Dominions discussion of defence policy. Australia and New Zealand, the Dominions who were most anxious for closer defence co-operation, were primarily concerned with obtaining satisfactory assurances from Britain about naval assistance in the event of trouble with Japan. However, at a more practical level, effective co-operation continued. The published conference report was able to note with satisfaction the adoption of a common system of organisation and training, and of the standardisation of equipment for Commonwealth naval, military and air forces. These forces could thus be intermeshed quickly in the event of war.

If the British wished to secure what they regarded as the essential Dominion support in any conflict with Germany, therefore, the avenue of appeasement would have to be explored to the full. Thus during the Munich crisis of September 1938, Chamberlain almost invariably received enthusiastic support from the Dominions – whose high commissioners were in daily contact in London with Malcom MacDonald, the Dominions Secretary – for the policy of seeking a settlement with Hitler over Czechoslovakia. As Smuts had written privately after the invasion of Austria in March 1938, 'the Dominions will fight for Great Britain if attacked, they will not fight in the battles of Central or South-Eastern Europe'.[35]

Support for the Munich agreement was therefore virtually unanimous in the British and Dominion cabinets; few wished to face the war which seemed the alternative to the rejection of Hitler's *diktat*. Even after the invasion of the rump of Czechoslovakia in

March 1939 had led to a reversal of British policy and the issuing of guarantees to Poland, there was Dominion reluctance to abandon the path of appeasement. As late as August 1939, British ministers could have cause for anxiety about Dominion hesitancy.

## SEPARATISM AND LOYALTY: THE DOMINIONS AND THE EMPIRE/COMMONWEALTH

It was only rarely that a specifically 'imperial' issue dominated local politics, as had happened in Britain during the Boer War. During the inter-war period, there were few such issues. Indian constitutional progress and 'Empire Free Trade' were both significant issues in British politics in the early 1930s, but the constitutional niceties of the Balfour definition were not the stuff of domestic political controversy. Dominion politicians, though they might like to cut a dash as imperial statesmen at the great Imperial Conferences of the period, were judged by their electorates on their performance at the parish pump. Thus Smuts, whose close involvement in the creation of the League of Nations established him as a statesman of worldwide reputation, was rejected by the South African electorate in 1924 and he was to suffer a similar fate in 1948, having achieved still greater distinction as an Allied leader during the Second World War.

There would of course be proper occasions for the manifestation of imperial sentiment, for example, in London when the conferences assembled, or in a Dominion visited by the Prince of Wales. Dominion leaders also appreciated, however, that there was some political mileage to be gained on occasion by a robust assertion of independence from British policy, as, for example, over the Chanak affair. The local political background against which inter-imperial relations were conducted was of especial significance in the case of those Dominions where significant anti-imperial sentiment existed. In the Irish Free State and the Union of South Africa, the two 'cuckoos in the imperial nest', membership of the Empire/ Commonwealth was a live domestic issue. Both countries were eventually to withdraw from the Commonwealth.

Dominion politics during the inter-war period were inevitably dominated by economic problems – most acute during the world depression of the early 1930s – and the social difficulties brought in their train. The smallest Dominion, Newfoundland, was even

forced by the threat of bankruptcy to abandon responsible government and to submit herself once more to 'direct rule' from London,
an alternative preferred by the Newfoundland parliament to union
with Canada. From 1934 until 1949, when Newfoundland became
the tenth province of Canada after the Newfoundland electorate
had voted in favour of confederation in a referendum, the country
was governed by commissioners under the supervision of the British
government. The Newfoundland experience was an object lesson to
those who favoured separatism in the larger federated Dominions.

We have seen how the depression forced Britain and the
Dominions, through the Ottawa Agreements, into an attempt at
closer economic co-operation. The nature of bilateral trading and
economic links between Britain and each Dominion during this
period must be understood in order to put into perspective the
equality of status doctrine proclaimed in the constitutional field.
Changes in constitutional formulae did not alter a dependent
relationship in the economic sphere. Of course this did not apply in
the case of Canada, where by 1930 United States investments far
outstripped those of Great Britain. Indeed Canadian Conservatives
such as R. B. Bennett (Prime Minister 1930–5) favoured closer
economic links with Britain and the Empire as an assertion of
economic independence in the face of the United States' domination
of the Canadian economy. As for South Africa, her huge mineral
resources had from Rhodes' time given her the ability to generate
capital for her own needs. Though economic ties with Britain were
very close, the relationship was one of inter-dependence rather than
dependence. As far as New Zealand, Australia and the Irish Free
State were concerned, however, their dependence on economic and
trading links with Britain during the inter-war period gave their
relationship with the mother country an almost 'neo-colonial'
character.

New Zealand relied on the British capital market for credit, and
her economy was totally dependent on the export of agricultural
products to the United Kingdom. As the value of her exports fell,
the debt burden became heavier. The price of butter nearly halved
in Britain between 1929 and 1935, and New Zealand dairy farmers
suffered accordingly, as of course did their counterparts in the
United Kingdom. New Zealand, however, had lessons to teach her
Commonwealth partners in the economic and social spheres. The
hardships of the depression years were softened by the commitment
of governments of both left and right to those progressive policies in

the fields of public health and social security which had distinguished the development of New Zealand society since the 1890s. In the field of race relations, too, New Zealand policy in the inter-war period, though not unblemished, compared very favourably with the treatment of non-whites in Australia, South Africa or even Canada. The Maori population of New Zealand had been decimated and ruthlessly deprived of their land as a result of the wars of the mid-nineteenth century. By the 1930s, however, Maoris were being encouraged by government grants to promote their own social and economic progress. The Maori population began to rise sharply again, and Maori culture gave a unique flavour to New Zealand society.

Most Australians also accepted the importance of the British connection, but the unequal relationship, particularly in the economic sphere, was keenly resented by elements in the powerful Australian Labour party. Like New Zealand, Australia faced the depression burdened by interest charges on debts from mainly British sources. Some left-wingers, such as J. T. Lang, the Prime Minister of New South Wales, favoured the repudiation of debt obligations owed to the 'plutocrats' in England. Apart from its dependence on British capital, Australia's pattern of trade with Britain followed that of New Zealand. Despite efforts to diversify her export trade and to promote the development of home-based manufacturing industry, agricultural products, mainly to Britain, still comprised 80 per cent of Australia's exports.

The relationship between Britain and Australia was complicated by the continuing intrusion of the 'imperial factor' into the federal Australian constitution. This arose from the anomalous position of the states, who cherished a direct relationship with Britain, symbolised by their agents-general in London and their British state governors, appointed without reference to the government in the new federal capital of Canberra. In 1933, the Westminster Parliament was embarrassed by a petition from Western Australia requesting that the state should be allowed to secede from the Commonwealth of Australia.

In the previous year, Australian Labour's suspicion of the British connection was aroused by the dismissal of the left-wing premier Lang by the governor of New South Wales. Forty-three years later Labour fury would know no bounds when the Labour federal Prime Minister, Gough Whitlam, was dismissed by the Governor-General, Sir John Kerr. Though both dismissals were purely domestic affairs, many Australian Labour Party supporters, not necessarily well-briefed on the niceties of constitutional theory, saw them as symbols of some lingering subordination to London.

A further indication of the limitations of equality of status in relation to Australia and New Zealand can be seen in the realms of defence and foreign affairs. In the 1930s, Australia supported Chamberlain's policy of the appeasement of Germany. It was obviously in Australia's interest that European quarrels should not deflect attention from the growing threat of Japanese expansion in Australia's 'near north'. The antipodean Dominions relied on Britain for their defence against this threat. The British navy's ability to provide the necessary assistance did not appear in doubt, in view of the completion of the new naval base at Singapore and the undertaking given at the 1937 Imperial Conference that any threat from Japan would be countered by the despatch of a fleet to the Far East.

Thus the real meaning of the Commonwealth link for Australia and New Zealand during this period was the consolidation of the special bilateral relationship with the 'Mother Country' to whom they were closely linked by ties of blood and on whom they were entirely dependent for their economic well-being and for the security of their shores. In the case of Canada and – to a much greater extent – South Africa, these bonds were perceptibly weaker.

Canada's security and prosperity depended on co-operation not with Britain but with her powerful neighbour, the United States; thus the latter's isolationism during this period was reflected in Canadian attitudes and policies towards the imperial connection. Moreover, like South Africa, Canada contained a substantial number of non-British European citizens. French-Canadian nationalism in Quebec revived strongly in the 1930s. Like their Afrikaner counterparts in South Africa, French-Canadian nationalist disliked the imperial connection as a symbol of their own domination by English-speaking Canadians, particularly those capitalists who controlled local trade and industry. The main concern, therefore, of William Lyon Mackenzie King, who created a Commonwealth record by holding office for twenty-three years during the period 1921–48, was to preserve the sometimes precarious unity of the Canadian confederation, a task which was sometimes eased by a display of awkwardness or self-assertiveness in an imperial context. King's political skill was exemplified by the political capital he was able to make out of the Chanak crisis and out of the refusal in 1926 of his request for a dissolution of parliament by Lord Byng, the British Governor-General.

French-Canadian nationalists could not hope to dominate the confederation. They could only aspire to some form of separation, and the fate of Newfoundland, as mentioned above, was not a happy augury for such a drastic move. In South Africa, however, the 'racial' conflict between Boer and Briton generated internal political and social conflict in the Union of a bitterness and intensity not found elsewhere in the Commonwealth. The huge non-white majority, almost completely excluded from participation in formal political activity, were treated as pawns in the struggle for hegemony between the European groups. In fact, the real racial issue in South Africa – that of relations between black and white – was already proving of key importance to the development of the modern Commonwealth. South Africa was the only self-governing Dominion with a predominantly non-European population. As we have seen, its record in the field of race relations did not inspire confidence in Indian nationalists in British undertakings regarding the political future of India as a 'brown dominion'.

South Africa in the inter-war years was a violent and troubled society. In the sphere of Anglo-Afrikaner relations alone, hopes expressed at the birth of the Union in 1910 that Boer and Briton would be reconciled to co-operation in the building of the new state were not to be fulfilled. Although the First World War, despite the 1914 rebellion, appeared to confirm the loyalty of the majority of Afrikaners to the Empire, the strength of Afrikaner nationalism was soon to be revealed. Smuts succeeded to the premiership on the death of Botha in 1919, but he soon faced a major political challenge from yet another ex-Boer general, J. B. M. Hertzog. The latter led the Afrikaner Nationalist Party, which was bitterly opposed to the Smuts–Botha policy of power-sharing with the English-speaking community. To those Afrikaners, still cherishing the humiliations of the Boer War and resentful of subsequent attempts to undermine Afrikaner culture, Hertzog's ideal of a reborn South African Republic made a strong appeal.

Smuts, although able in 1921 to achieve a merger of his South African Party and the smaller, English-speaking Unionist Party, lost his majority in the 1924 general election. He lacked Botha's 'gracious patience' with his own people. Hampered by Smuts's long absences abroad on 'imperial business', the government had been beset by industrial problems at home. Hertzog was able to form a government with the support of the South African Labour Party, the political mouthpiece of the white mineworkers with whom the Smuts government had clashed so bitterly during major strikes and disturbances on the Rand in 1922. This apparently incongruous alliance of parties representing respectively the Afrikaner farmer and the mainly English-speaking miners was cemented by hatred of Smuts and of the capitalist 'Randlords'. Both parties could agree on a programme designed to strengthen still further the economic and political position of whites in South Africa. The nationalists also sniped at the imperial connection by sponsoring the introduction of a new flag to replace the Union Jack, and more seriously began what was to be a long-drawn-out campaign against the retention of the non-European franchise in Cape Province, the only 'liberal' element in the Union constitution as far as the non-white inhabitants were concerned.

Although the Nationalists won an absolute majority in the 1929 general election, the economic difficulties associated with the world slump, and divisions within his own party, led Hertzog to accept Smuts's offer of coalition in 1933. In the following year, the Nationalist and South African parties fused as the 'United Party'. As in Hertzog's own case before the First World War, however, compromise was unacceptable to some Afrikaners, and a group of 'purified nationalists' under Dr Malan broke away from the coalition to form the basis of the party which was eventually to defeat Smuts in 1948. Nevertheless, the United Party had a strong nationalist flavour about it. The Status of the Union Act, 1934, which adopted the Statute of Westminster as part of the law of South Africa, declared South Africa to be a 'sovereign independent state', and Hertzog had already made it clear that he would insist on the Union's right to remain neutral in any future war in which Britain might be involved.

In the field of 'native' affairs, Smuts acquiesced in two further important measures towards the achievement of complete political and territorial segregation between black and white, the Native Trust and Land Act, and the Representation of Natives Act, 1936. This latter measure, which removed native voters from the common electoral roll in the Cape, was strongly opposed by Jan Hofmeyr, one of Smuts's closest colleagues. His stand, however attracted negligible support in parliament. The influence of the Cape liberal tradition was weakening in the face of overwhelming electoral support for the entrenchment of white supremacy and the elimination of any possibility of competition from the African majority.

That majority, even if deprived of any effective 'legitimate' political voice, was by no means silent. The South African Native National Congress organised protests against the Pass Laws, and Clements Kadalie's Industrial and Commercial Workers Union organised strikes and demonstrations. In 1920, 40,000 African miners struck on the Rand, and during the period immediately after the First World War, labour unrest – strikes, riots and boycotts – was endemic among the coloured and African populations of the cities. When this unrest is seen in conjunction with the appalling violence associated with the white miners' strike of 1922, when martial law was declared and there were 687 casualties, including 152 Africans, some impression of the tensions within South African society emerges. Despite immense mineral wealth – by 1939 the country's annual output of gold was worth almost £100 million – prosperity without social justice gave little assurance for the future.

Despite Smuts' personal stature as an international philosopher-statesman, South Africa's image abroad suffered. Though successful in obtaining a League of Nations' Mandate – which in effect meant complete control – over the former German colony of South West Africa in 1919, the Union's other plans for territorial expansion were not realised. In 1922 the white voters of Southern Rhodesia declined (by 8774 votes to 5989) to join the Union on terms which Smuts had negotiated with the retiring administrators, the British South Africa Company. Nor were successive South African governments able to persuade the British government to transfer to the Union the three 'High Commission' territories of Bechuanaland, Basutoland and Swaziland.

If Whitehall was tempted to yield to General Hertzog's blandishments, a strong campaign by the British 'native interests' lobby led by Lord Lugard and Margery Perham procured the shelving of the issue. As Margery Perham wrote in *The Times*, it was impossible to consider the treatment of these territories apart from the whole question of South African native policy.[36] After the Second World War, that policy was to become of increasing significance in South Africa's relations with her Commonwealth partners.

Finally, there was the Irish Free State, the newest and most reluctant Dominion. We have seen that in Canada, Australia and New Zealand the weakening bonds of Empire were not regarded as too irksome and, indeed, were still widely cherished despite resentment among some French nationalists and Australian labour leaders. Even in South Africa, although the 'purified' nationalists nursed an abiding hatred of the Empire/Commonwealth, most Afrikaners were prepared to follow General Hertzog, who, while clinging to the republican ideal, was prepared to accept that the 1926 Balfour definition (which he had played a dominant part in drafting) permitted the full realisation of the political, cultural and economic aspirations of the *Volk* within a Commonwealth framework.

Ireland was different. In Ulster, the Protestant majority wished to remain politically united with the rest of the United Kingdom. They accepted the limited self-government provided for by the Government of Ireland Act 1920 without enthusiasm, except in so far as it preserved them from absorption into a Catholic-dominated united Ireland. As far as the rest of Ireland was concerned, the 1918 election had established clearly that the republican Sinn Fein movement had effective political control of the population. But only after three years of intermittent warfare, characterised by atrocities on both sides, was the British government brought to concede Dominion status to the 'Irish Free State' in the Anglo-Irish treaty of 1921. This agreement ensured that, generally, the position of the Free State in relation to the Imperial Parliament and Government should be that of the Dominion of Canada.

Southern Ireland, however, could not take her place cosily as one of the daughter nations of the Commonwealth. Ireland was herself a mother country, not a colony of settlement, the source of the large 'Irish' communities in North America and Australia. Her leaders did not acknowledge any debt of gratitude to Britain for the concession of Irish freedom, no 'miracle of trust and magnanimity' such as had reconciled defeated Boer leaders in South Africa. The Irish considered that they had won their freedom by force of arms, as was recognised implicitly by the negotiation of the 'treaty' in 1921. To them the British imperial system was the hated instrument of oppression, so long the denial of their national freedom. There were no 'Commonwealth men', in the southern Irish leadership, sentimentally attached to the Crown and other imperial symbols. Indeed, so objectionable were those symbols to many Sinn Feiners that a bitter civil war was fought in 1922 before the 'Treaty party' triumphed. The republican leader, Eammon de Valera, always maintained that Dominion status was imposed by Britain by the threat of force in 1921, and when he became Prime Minister in

1932, he devoted himself towards severing the last formal links between southern Ireland and the Commonwealth.

Even the 'Free Staters' did not accept Dominion status as a full satisfaction of Irish national aspirations, but rather as a staging post on the road to freedom. Thus, in the years before de Valera came to power, the Irish played a dynamic role in imperial deliberations in the 'status push' which removed the lingering anomalies of subordination between Britain and her fellow Commonwealth members. Ironically, therefore, Ireland, destined soon to leave the Commonwealth, helped to fashion it in a way which could accommodate the national aspirations of its diverse peoples. Under de Valera, southern Ireland adopted the constitution of 1937 which made her a republic in all but name, and though links with the Commonwealth were not ended formally until 1949, Irish neutrality in 1939 meant the 'severing of all intimate Commonwealth communications and relations between the governments'.[37]

The Anglo-Irish treaty may be regarded symbolically as the first major concession to the rising tide of nationalism which, from Egypt, India and elsewhere was soon to engulf the British imperial system. However, Anglo-Irish relations have always been *sui generis*. Just as before 1921 it was unthinkable to many Englishmen that Irish national aspirations should be satisfied by destroying the hard-won political unity of the British Isles – thus undoing, as the great Victorian lawyer A. V. Dicey put it, 'the work not only of Pitt, but of Somers, of Henry VII, and of Edward I' – so after 1921, or even after 1949, Britain and southern Ireland remained bound together by geography, population exchange and economics, bonds of a kind which do not exist between Britain and any of her Commonwealth partners. Yet in 1921 the blow at the heart of the Empire, though largely symbolic, had been keenly felt, and had awoken the fears expressed so forcibly during the 1886 Irish Home Rule Bill crisis by Joseph Chamberlain and other convinced unionists and imperialists.

# PART 4

# THE SECOND WORLD WAR AND
# ITS AFTERMATH, 1939–51

## THE EMPIRE'S WAR, 1939–41

When Britain entered the Second World War the Commonwealth/
Empire was larger in terms of territory and population than in 1914.
It was also much more fragile and disaffected. The Indian
subcontinent seethed with unrest, and complete independence
seemed within the grasp of Indian nationalists. In Egypt (which was
formally independent) the continuing presence of a British garrison
under the terms of the 1936 Treaty remained a source of nationalist
indignation. The mandated territory of Palestine threatened to
become ungovernable as the antagonism between Jews and Arabs
deepened. Cyprus was impatient with British rule. Ceylon had
achieved the substance of domestic autonomy. Even within West
Indian and African colonies there were the first flickerings of
movements for self-government.

The white Dominions, for so long the prefects of the imperial
system, no longer overflowed with loyalty for king and country. The
Irish Free State had already, in all but name, abandoned Dominion
status. In South Africa the coalition government of General
Hertzog, relying heavily on Afrikaner support, was an extremely
doubtful ally. Inter-war relations between Canada and Britain,
though generally cordial, had not been exclusively so, and French-
Canadians had found no fresh reasons to love the British crown and
the British government. Australia and New Zealand were still
deeply dependent upon the British connection, especially in the
fields of commerce and defence, but their total combined population was less than 10,000,000.[1]

Nor were the circumstances of the outbreak of war in September
1939 likely to arouse universal enthusiasm throughout the Empire.
Following Hitler's invasion of the Czech Republic in March 1939,

81

the British and French governments had guaranteed Poland's independence. How these guarantees were to be honoured without a parallel alliance with the Soviet Union was not, however, clear. Still, Nazi Germany had been given the firmest indication to date that Britain and France would oppose further eastward expansion. Perhaps doubting Anglo-French resolve, and having secured a non-aggression treaty with Russia in August, Hitler invaded Poland on 1 September 1939. After momentary hesitation, Neville Chamberlain's government, faced with an uncompromising majority in the House of Commons, declared war on 3 September. A somewhat reluctant France followed her ally into the affray.

The preservation of Poland's sovereignty was not essential to Britain's imperial interests. It is indeed arguable that Hitler was genuine when he claimed that he had no designs on the British Empire. Once Germany had acquired her *lebensraum* (living space) in eastern Europe and the Ukraine, it was quite conceivable that her ambitions would not include the acquisition of an Empire that was already difficult to govern. The Second World War had its roots firmly in the soil of Europe, and at first appeared to be well removed from Indian and African, and even Canadian, interests.

To some, Britain's involvement in the conflict seemed a quixotic gesture, lacking in real meaning. Britain had co-operated with totalitarian and autocratic governments in the past. Although the anti-semitic activities of the Nazi regime were deeply repugnant to many, they did not in themselves provide the justification for declaring war – rather they added fuel to subsequent anti-Nazi propaganda. It was also difficult (as in 1914–18) for the British government to proclaim a crusade for freedom when full political freedoms were simultaneously withheld in large parts of the Empire.

In the event, the Empire's reaction to the war was predictably varied. Australia and New Zealand considered themselves bound by the mother country's declaration of war; in this respect Australasian dependence upon Britain's defence system in South East Asia and the South Pacific was no doubt as potent a factor as traditional loyalty. Canada, as befitted the senior Dominion, availed herself of the right to defer any decision to her own parliament. When the Canadian House of Commons met a week after the outbreak of war it declared itself unanimously for entering the hostilities.

In South Africa the Nationalist Prime Minister Hertzog hoped to remain neutral. A resolution to this effect was put before the Union parliament at Cape Town, but an amendment by Smuts, which was pro-British and anti-German, obtained a majority of thirteen. Failing to secure a dissolution of parliament from the Governor-General, Sir Patrick Duncan, Hertzog resigned and Smuts, ever eager to don uniform, took over the premiership. However, Afrikaner opposition to the war was considerable. The purified Nationalists, led by Malan and Strijdom, were unashamedly pro-Nazi; the government interned some of these extremists, including three future prime ministers of South Africa. For good measure, some communists were also interned.[2]

The Irish Free State proved that the Statute of Westminster was no hollow statement of Dominion sovereignty by declaring itself neutral.[3] It maintained a meticulous official neutrality throughout the conflict, even though there could be little doubt which side the de Valera government wanted to win, and recent evidence suggests that it would have accepted British assistance in the event of a German invasion. In practical terms the Free State's decision denied the Royal Navy the use of its southern Irish bases, which would have been useful during the war against the U-boats. Official neutrality did not, however, prevent thousands of Irishmen from joining the United Kingdom's forces. Ulster was, of course, part of the United Kingdom, yet the republican sympathies of its large Catholic minority meant that the British government exempted the six northern counties from conscription.

If the Dominions' reaction to the outbreak of war was ambiguous, so was India's. The Viceroy (Lord Linlithgow) simply announced that war had broken out between the King-Emperor and Germany. No democratic process was followed. The Muslim League was prepared to accept Britain's decision, but, although the Congress party in general disliked Nazi Germany, the official British attitude to India's involvement in the war rankled. In the provinces, indeed, the Congress ministries resigned in protest, and the Indian Civil Service resumed the traditional administrative duties that it had so recently abandoned.[4]

It was soon evident that Britain could not hold down India and fight a war against Hitler's Germany. Perhaps logistical considerations were more powerful than ethical ones. At any rate, Churchill's coalition government gave an undertaking that India's post-war constitution would be determined by an elected constituent assembly. There was much irony in this. In the 1930s, as we have seen, Churchill had fought tooth and nail against concessions to Indian nationalism; on assuming the premiership he had announced 'I have not become First Minister of the Crown in order to preside over the liquidation of the British Empire'. Now even a government led by Churchill was prepared to smooth the way towards Indian independence.

The war saw other significant advances in colonial policy. In 1940 the Colonial Development and Welfare Act was introduced: it set aside £5,000,000 a year for promoting development schemes in the colonial empire. This was a bounty that would previously have been unthinkable except as a response to some local disaster, and indicated a far greater commitment to colonial economic development.[5] The franchise in Jamaica and the Gold Coast was extended during the war, thus partly paving the way to post-war independence. Above all, the recruitment of Africans and West Indians into the imperial forces on a scale unknown in the Great War meant that these colonial citizens had their horizons (and perhaps their political ambitions) widened.

In the Middle East and North Africa, Commonwealth forces had achieved some success by December 1941. The Italians had been thrown out of Ethiopia and Italian Somaliland. The Suez Canal was still safe, even though the nominally neutral government of Egypt had shown itself unenthusiastic for a war against Italy. The Palestine mandate, however, continued to be an embarrassment to Britain, for while the Jews hated Nazi Germany, the Arabs (faced with militant Zionism) were not wholly unsympathetic towards an avowedly anti-semitic regime.[6]

Iraq was a further complication for British policy-makers, since an anti-British regime had been set up in 1941 and wished to eliminate the Royal Air Force base and with it British influence. The value of Iraq as a source of oil and a channel for communication with Soviet Russia prompted a British invasion in 1943, and Iraq subsequently entered the war on the side of the Allies. An Anglo-Russian partition of Persia (on the lines of the spheres of influence established in 1907) cordoned off yet more territory from Axis influence. But though by the end of 1941 the British Empire was still intact, military disaster was, in fact, imminent.

## WORLD WAR, 1941–45

The Japanese air attack on the American naval base of Pearl Harbor in December 1941 effectively won the war for the British

Empire. The immense military potential of the United States was now thrown into the balance against Germany, Italy and Japan. The Grand Alliance between Britain, Russia and the United States seemed assured of ultimate victory. Even the assault on Pearl Harbor had been a failure in one important respect, since the American aircraft carriers (the key to the naval struggle in the Pacific) had escaped destruction.

The months after Pearl Harbor, however, saw the collapse of much of the British imperial structure in the Far East. Hong Kong fell on Christmas day 1941, Malaya was invaded (via Indo-China), and the sinking of the *Prince of Wales* and the *Repulse* destroyed the pretensions of the navy as a bastion of British imperial power in the East. In February 1942, with a crash that shook the Empire to its foundations, the great fortress of Singapore fell, almost without a struggle; nearly 100,000 British, Australian and New Zealand troops were captured. The Japanese swept through Burma and reached the frontiers of India; they took British, Dutch, American and French possessions in the Pacific, and thus extended their power uncomfortably close to Australia and New Zealand.[7]

Britain's imperial prestige was now in shreds. An Asiatic nation had ripped the far-eastern Empire apart. Comfortable (indeed necessary) assumptions of European supremacy could never be entirely re-established. The effective destruction of the British naval presence in far-eastern waters had taken a few minutes: Australia and New Zealand would have to look elsewhere for their protection. The Japanese success confused many Asian nationalist leaders; some saw the Japanese as liberators; Gandhi argued that the British must now quit India so that a purified subcontinent could face Japan with more hope of success. Other Indian nationalist leaders, however, did not wish to exchange British overlordship for domination by Japan.

Nonetheless the British government considered it vital to stabilise the position in India. Churchill therefore dispatched a mission headed by the (Christian) socialist Stafford Cripps to talk to Congress and Muslim League leaders. Military expediency, and perhaps American pressure, caused this initiative. Churchill found little joy in the mission and in some ways did his best to sabotage it.[8] Cripps proposed terms that amounted to post-war independence (within or outside the Empire), the right of contracting-out for the Muslim provinces, and the immediate inclusion of nationalist leaders on the Viceroy's Council. After seriously considering these proposals, Congress decided to reject them.

In so doing, Congress also passed the famous 'Quit India' resolution and called for the immediate dismantling of the Raj. No British government could do such a thing in mid-1942, with the war still far from won. The Congress leadership was arrested, and a wave of violent protest, described by the Viceroy Lord Linlithgow as 'the worst since the Mutiny', swept the country. Order was restored, and eventually Field Marshal Sir Archibald Wavell replaced Linlithgow, but not before Ali Jinnah's Muslim League had passed its 'Divide and Quit' resolution; it was to prove a prophetic demand.[9]

Throughout the occupied territories of the Empire the Japanese impact was ambiguous. Burmese nationalists at first welcomed the British defeat, but later turned against the Japanese. In Malaya, Borneo and Hong Kong, the eventual British reconquest met little pro-Japanese resistance. Perhaps this was due to the abrupt self-interest of Japanese rule; the South-East Asia Co-Prosperity Sphere seemed little better than British imperialism, and in some respects distinctly worse.

The war had damaged Britain's imperial standing in other ways. After 1941 the Soviet Union and the United States bore an increasing share of the war effort. Neither of these powers were particularly friendly towards British imperialism; the Soviet government disliked the Empire from conviction based on theory, the Americans from habit. In some respects President Roosevelt was as inclined to trust Stalin as Winston Churchill. This meant that neither Russia nor the United States considered it their duty to help maintain the British Empire, though by the end of the war the Americans, suddenly anxious to prevent the spread of communism, were more cautious in their anti-imperialist attitudes.[10]

Within the United Kingdom itself the rigours of total war led many of its citizens to look for reforms and radical change when peace came. With three out of seven buildings damaged by bombing, with the memories of inter-war unemployment and economic hardship still fresh, the electorate wanted social improvement rather than imperial posturing. Between the defeat of Germany and Japan, therefore, the 1945 general election returned a Labour government with an overwhelming majority. As a whole, the Labour party was by no means composed of dedicated anti-imperialists, but it certainly contained such elements. In this respect, the new masters of the Empire were markedly different from their predecessors, despite the wartime tendency towards bipartisanship in such matters as colonial development.

## THE LABOUR GOVERNMENT AND THE EMPIRE, 1945–51

The Labour administration led by Clement Attlee inherited an economy bled white by five years of global war. Britain was massively in debt (chiefly to the United States) and her export trade was 40 per cent of its pre-war total. The material fruits of victory were not much in evidence. In these circumstances, the government had to concentrate its major efforts on domestic matters; the Empire did not rank high on its list of priorities.[11]

But there were certain obligations to fulfil. The most pressing was the establishment of Indian independence. The Attlee government had no desire to renege on the undertaking of the wartime coalition to grant India self-rule, nor indeed was there any practical way in which it could have done so. The mechanics of withdrawal, however, were complicated by the growing communal tensions in the subcontinent. Post-war elections to the central and provincial legislatures had shown sweeping gains by the Muslim League. Jinnah was confident that an independent state of Pakistan could be set up, and he was not prepared to consider an all-India federation with home rule in the Hindu and Muslim provinces.[12]

Serious rioting in the summer of 1946 prompted the British government to recall Wavell and appoint Lord Mountbatten of Burma as the last Viceroy. Mountbatten brought the prestige of his royal connections and his war record to his new post (he had been Supreme Allied Commander in South-East Asia); he had in addition a well-developed diplomatic sense and the capacity for decision-making. He also saw eye to eye with the Attlee government on a good many issues.[13]

On his appointment, Mountbatten set a time limit beyond which Britain would no longer administer India. His original date was June 1948. After his arrival in India in March 1947, he advanced the date of withdrawal to August 1947. The leaders of Congress and the Muslim League joined in a temporary administration to supervise partition. A boundary commission moved rapidly round the subcontinent delineating the two new states of India and

Pakistan. In July 1947 the India Independence Act was rushed through Parliament in a week. On 15 August the Union Jacks that had flown for so long over the subcontinent were hauled down, and the regiments that had hitherto kept the flags flying embarked for home. The British had built up their position in India over a period of three hundred years, but they finally abandoned it in a few weeks.[14]

Pakistan was formed out of East Bengal, the western Punjab, Sind and Baluchistan. Between East and West Pakistan lay a thousand miles of Indian territory. Some 80,000,000 people eventually found themselves in Pakistan, 320,000,000 in India. The approach of independence saw massive migrations of Hindus from territory designated to Pakistan, and of Muslims from Indian territory. Violent communal hatreds and fears resulted in the horrendous massacre of many refugees; perhaps a quarter of a million died in the tumult. Princely India collapsed once the bayonets of the Raj were withdrawn. Maharajas, Rajas and Nizams joined the most appropriate of the new states. But the great province of Hyderabad had to be subdued by the Indian army, and most of Kashmir (the homeland of Nehru) albeit with a Muslim majority was dragged into the new India only after bitter fighting with Pakistani forces.

In Pakistan, Ali Jinnah became Governor-General with Liaquat Ali Khan as his Prime Minister. Mountbatten served briefly as Governor-General of the Dominion of India where Nehru became Prime Minister. Gandhi, who had mobilised the masses behind Congress and had campaigned to the last to avoid communal violence, was assassinated by a Hindu extremist five months after independence. Jinnah died towards the end of 1949.[15]

With the abandonment of the Indian Empire, both Burma and Ceylon were granted independence. Burma had never allowed the British fully to reinstate themselves after the defeat of the Japanese. Now a general election resulted in a huge majority in favour of immediate independence. In January 1948 Burma became a republic and left the Commonwealth. To the south of the subcontinent, Ceylon, a month later, became a Dominion within the Commonwealth. Ceylon's path to independence had been relatively smooth and, in many respects, unique. The liberal and democratic Donoughmore constitution of 1931 had led to complete independence within two decades.

In order to accommodate India's demand for republican status within the Commonwealth, the British government produced a new formula in consultation with the Commonwealth Prime Ministers at the conference of 1949. The chief innovation was the description of the monarch as 'Head of the Commonwealth'.[16] It was appropriate that within two years of its independence India, so long the fulcrum of British imperial interests, should have trimmed the title of the British sovereign in this way. The episode was indeed a clear sign of the changed times.

The 1949 formula appeared at the time as another triumph for British-style compromise; a fresh demonstration of the strength and flexibility of the Commonwealth. However, in addition to the final departure in the same year of the Republic of Ireland, for a generation the most recalcitrant of the Dominions, there had been a real weakening of the Commonwealth – now not even the 'British' Commonwealth – as an instrument of Britain's imperial purpose. No longer united by 'a common allegiance to the Crown', the fundamental principle enshrined in the Balfour Definition of 1926 and obstinately clung to in the long wrangle with southern Ireland, members now agreed only to co-operate in 'the pursuit of peace, liberty and progress' – whatever that might mean. The accommodation of republican India within the Commonwealth also opened the way to a new South African Republic, the dream of the Afrikaner National Party which had decisively defeated Smuts in the 1948 general election.

The declaration of London contained no reference to military security or political co-operation. However, before the war S. M. Bruce of Australia had referred to the 'unwritten treaty of mutual guarantee' between Commonwealth members, and during the war the Commonwealth (except for southern Ireland whose membership was then in name only) had functioned as a political and military alliance. Now, however, independent India had embraced a policy of 'non-alignment', and participated in public attacks on British 'imperialism'. As we have seen, the old 'family' had been disrupted further by armed conflict between the quarrelling new members, India and Pakistan. Yet in the view of Patrick Gordon Walker: 'The years 1950-1951 marked a high point in the co-ordination of strategy and foreign policy in the Commonwealth'.[17]

The most remarkable demonstration of this was the formation of the 'Commonwealth Division' to fight in Korea; it consisted of troops from Britain, Canada, Australia, New Zealand, an Indian ambulance unit, and an integrated staff, including South African officers. The real interests of the post-war security, however, had fundamentally diminished the importance of inter-Commonwealth co-operation in this field. The 'British Empire' was no longer a superpower with the ability to act independently in world affairs, whatever appearances might still suggest. In Europe and North America the security of Britain and Canada depended on the United States, through membership of the North Atlantic Treaty Organisation. In the Far East, where the communist threat had soon replaced that of the Japanese, the events of 1942 had destroyed the pretensions of the British imperial defence system to protect Australia and New Zealand. The latter could look only to the United States, with whom the ANZUS Pact was concluded in 1951. Britain, despite her protests, was excluded from this arrangement, since the United States did not wish to be involved in the support of British colonial commitments in Asia.

No longer an effective political or military alliance, the post-war importance of the Commonwealth appeared to lie in economic and financial co-operation. As Britain's relative share of world trade declined, the imperial proportion of Britain's trade increased: for the years 1946–9, the Empire/Commonwealth provided 48 per cent of her imports and took 57.5 per cent of her exports. By comparison, Europe handled only 25 per cent of Britain's trade. Armed with these facts, Ernest Bevin, Labour's Foreign Secretary, told a TUC audience in 1947 that a European Customs Union was of little interest to Britain, and that his personal preference would be for a customs union of the Commonwealth.[18]

There was now no prospect of turning Joseph Chamberlain's old dream into reality, but the scheme of imperial preference introduced at Ottawa in 1932 survived post-war United States' opposition to what they chose to regard as trade discrimination. The launching of the Colombo Plan in 1950 suggested, moreover, that the Commonwealth could play a leading role in promoting the economic progress of underdeveloped areas such as south-east Asia.

In the financial field, however, the relative weakness of Britain after the war meant that the maintenance of sterling as a 'great international currency' and particularly as a kind of imperial currency of the Commonwealth had become a burden rather than a benefit to the mother country. During the war, India and the Dominions had built up huge sterling balances which were, in effect, debts owed by the United Kingdom to other members of the sterling area. Ironically however, Britain's debtor position gave her a bargaining strength in monetary dealings with her sterling partners who had to submit to strict management of the system by the British Treasury. Even the massive devaluation of the pound sterling against the dollar in September 1949 (by over 30 per cent from $4.03 to $2.80) – in other ways a sad symptom of Britain's economic decline – was weathered by the sterling 'club', and all the other members devalued their currencies in line with the pound.

As regards the dependent Empire, the granting of independence to India, Pakistan, Burma and Ceylon and the rather ignominious abandonment of the troublesome Palestine mandate in 1948 need not be seen as the first fruits of a Labour commitment to decolonisation, but as 'the letting go of what, after a war, just could not be held'.[19] Certainly there was to be no wholesale retreat from colonial responsibilities, a course ruled out on the grounds of both idealism and self-interest.

Before the war, the Labour leader Clement Attlee had spoken of Labour's commitment to the 'abandonment of imperialism' in the colonies. This meant, not the end of colonial rule in colonies which in most cases were seen even in 1945 as generations away from self-government, but the ending of the exploitation of colonial peoples in the economic sphere and its replacement by development policies which would put real flesh on the old bones of trusteeship. Fabian improvement was to come to the colonies, as illustrated by the almost Rousseau-esque flavour of a 1946 Colonial Office mem-orandum on mining policy which spoke of minerals as 'the gift of nature' for the benefit of the community at large.[20]

The idea of colonial development was, of course, not new. It went back, as we have seen, to the pre-war period, and had become orthodox doctrine not only among Labour colonial pundits, but also among the ranks of progressive Conservative politicians such as Oliver Stanley, the wartime Colonial Secretary, and among enlightened officials such as Andrew Cohen, later to be a con-troversial governor of Uganda. Labour in fact followed the path laid down by the Colonial Development and Welfare Act of 1940 and its successor in 1945, both products of the wartime coalition. Although effective progress was made in the building of schools, hospitals, roads and so on, the more elaborate schemes were not always successful – the notorious groundnut scheme left thousands of pounds' worth of machinery rusting in the Tanganyika bush.

Underlying the story of the success or failure of a particular project, however, the policy of colonial development itself cannot be separated from the stresses and ambiguities of the final phase of

Empire. The last generation of imperial administrators, led by men like Andrew Cohen and Arthur Creech Jones, Labour's Colonial Secretary from 1946 to 1950, were above all anxious to further the interests of the peoples in their charge. They set about their task with admirable energy and idealism, and the once moribund Colonial Office became a dynamic and progressive institution.

Yet the British Empire, even 'Labour's Empire', remained essentially an institution for the maintenance of Britain's economic and political position as a world power, and as in reality that power declined, the colonies appeared to have an increasingly vital supporting role. The Empire did not become a charitable institution devoted solely to the benefit of the colonial peoples. Rather the emphasis lay in the mobilisation of the economic resources of the colonial Empire – in particular raw materials such as Malayan rubber, Northern Rhodesian copper, and the food and vegetable oil products of west Africa – to help the struggling British economy and to close the notorious 'dollar gap', the bane of post-war Chancellors of the Exchequer.

Where Britain's priorities lay was indicated by the massive expenditure on defence with which post-war governments sought to sustain Britain's pretensions to remain a 'great power'. Colonial development programmes could not compete with the atomic bomb, the Berlin airlift or Korea. Despite the worthy endeavours of Creech Jones and his associates, colonies only made political news at home when there was some kind of trouble such as the Seretse Khama affair,[21] the Gold Coast riots of 1948, or the Malayan emergency of the same year. The latter began a twelve-year struggle against a small number of communist insurgents in the Malayan jungle, thus showing the defence of the 'imperial frontier' might still take priority when consistent with Anglo-American Cold War strategy.

The troubles in the Gold Coast in 1948, however, were a warning that Fabian improvement within the traditional authoritarian political structure would not satisfy the aspirations of the emerging nationalist leadership in the 'backward' tropical dependencies in Africa, where the problem of political advance was to dominate the imperial scene in the 1950s and 60s as effectively as had the Indian quest for self-government in the period up to 1947. As in the case of India, Africa was to prove a puzzle which policy-makers in London were painfully slow to unravel, perhaps because they were very reluctant to recognise the legitimacy of the local black nationalist leadership. While the Colonial Office had recognised the need to come to terms with local nationalism in the West Indies by the concession of semi-responsible government and universal suffrage in Jamaica in 1944, Africa was thought to be in a quite different stage of political development. Self-government, it was agreed, could only come through the gradual evolution of those institutions of indirect rule so lovingly created between the wars.

As far as east and central Africa were concerned, Labour ministers felt it their duty to prevent a complete transfer of power into the hands of local European settlers on the Southern Rhodesian model. They accepted, however, that European settlers had an essential role to play in the development of territories like Kenya in a way which would make African political progress possible. The Europeans of Kenya thus gained considerable concessions during Labour's period of office. In 1946 the Kenya government announced plans for expanded European settlement in the 'white' Highlands, and Labour's Colonial Secretary robustly refused to open up these areas to non-European settlement. In the following year, the Europeans achieved an unofficial majority in the Legislative Council. However, 1946 had also seen the return to Kenya after a long absence in England of Jomo Kenyatta, bent on the task of turning African nationalist sentiment into an effective political force.[22]

For Kenyatta many years of struggle lay ahead, but Kwame Nkrumah, another exile, returning in 1947 was to find himself within ten years the Prime Minister of the first black independent member of the Commonwealth – the former west African colony of the Gold Coast. West Africa of course was recognised as being more 'advanced' than the east and central African dependencies – there had been unofficial African representation in the Gold Coast Legislative Council since 1888, and in 1946 the territory acquired the first Legislative Council in British Africa with a majority of African members. The rapidity of subsequent constitutional progress reflected the strength of local nationalist pressure which became progressively more difficult to resist. Serious riots in the capital, Accra, in 1948 were at first blamed on communist influence. A wide-ranging commission of enquiry (the Watson Commission) was set up and recommended increased African political responsibility as the solution to the country's problems. As a result an all-African committee under Mr Justice Coussey was established to make detailed constitutional recommendations.[23]

The new constitution, which came into force in 1951, resulted in a sweeping electoral victory for Nkrumah's Convention People's Party, which had been founded in 1949 as a mass movement to press for immediate self-government and which rejected the gradualist approach of the established local political leadership. Nkrumah, whose agitation had placed him behind the bars of a colonial prison (later to be accepted as a 'normal' experience for an aspiring nationalist politician in Africa) was released to assume political office, firstly as 'leader of government business'. That euphemism, however, was soon dropped, and in 1952 Nkrumah became Prime Minister, soon to be in political charge of a colony with full internal self-government.

Political change was also accelerated in Nigeria. A new constitution introduced in 1947, and designed for revision after nine years, was, in fact, replaced in 1951 by arrangements providing for an African majority in the Council of Ministers. The problems of regional rivalry in so vast a country were later to create special obstacles to constitutional progress, but by the time the British Labour government fell from office in 1951, it was clear that a rapid advance to Nigerian self-government was inevitable.

# PART 5

# THE COMMONWEALTH IN TRANSITION, 1951–65

The thirteen-year period of Conservative government in Britain which began in 1951 saw the transformation of the Commonwealth as an institution and the effective end of Britain's role as an imperial power. These two processes were linked in that one of the principal factors affecting the Commonwealth was the large increase in membership brought about by the admission of twelve newly independent former British dependencies – ten of which were inhabited mainly by non-Europeans. The withdrawal of South Africa, one of the 'old Dominions', in 1961 was also a significant indication of the extent of the changes that were taking place. The startling rapidity of Britain's retreat from Empire requires consideration and explanation before we turn to the nature of the Commonwealth relationship.

## THE DEPENDENT EMPIRE: THE 'WIND OF CHANGE'

It may seem ironic that a Conservative administration, led initially by the imperialist stalwart Winston Churchill, was in power during a period when Britain gave up the bulk of her colonial Empire for which, even after the transfer of power in India, she had seemed likely to remain responsible for some decades. It is difficult, of course, to see how any British government could have prevented the break-up of the Empire or, indeed, even justified the retention of the imperial commitments which had been retained in the aftermath of the Second World War.

By the 1950s, Britain had ceased to be an economic and political power of the first rank, as was dramatically illustrated by the collapse of her attempt to act independently of the United States in the Suez crisis of 1956. Resistance to independence movements all over the globe would make enormous demands on Britain's resources, which were more urgently needed to improve living standards and renovate industry at home. In any case, many outposts of Empire had rather a redundant air now that India, the 'brightest jewel', was gone. Nevertheless, it was not easy for the Conservative Party to adjust itself to the diminution of Britain's imperial power. Hence the anxiety of the leadership to present the transformation of the old dependent Empire into the new Commonwealth as some kind of new triumph for British statesmanship; the working out of a time-hallowed plan by which the territories had been prepared for self-government.[1]

Yet a real dilemma remained where this process appeared to conflict with vital British interests – the control of key natural resources or a strategic base – or the interests of local settler communities of predominately British stock. Moreover, as the pace quickened, the time-scale for the period of preparation for self-government became so truncated as to defy justification under any theory of colonial administration, save that of expediency.

This dilemma was expressed in the uneven response of the Conservative government in the 1950s to problems of what was once called 'imperial policy'. As Oliver Lyttleton, Colonial Secretary from 1951–4, has written:

> . . . it seemed clear that the development of self-government . . . was at once the only enlightened and the only practical theme of a colonial policy in the nineteen-fifties[2]

Thus with apparent good grace, the British government assisted the transition to full independence in the Gold Coast which, as we have seen, became the new sovereign state of Ghana in 1957. In the same year, the vast and unwieldy Federation of Nigeria acquired an African Prime Minister and went on to achieve full independence in 1960. There was therefore no interruption of the constitutional course which had been set under the Attlee government. Both Ghana and Nigeria at first remained as monarchies within the Commonwealth, and the British could reasonably congratulate themselves that power had been transferred into what seemed mature and responsible hands.

The former Anglo-Egyptian condominium of the Sudan had already achieved a peaceful transition to independence at the beginning of 1956. Although for fifty-seven years Britain had been in sole effective control of the Sudan, the Egyptians hoped, mistakenly, that Sudan would opt for union with Egypt. The Sudanese problem had involved some delicate negotiations with the revolutionary regime which had ousted King Farouk from the Egyptian throne in 1952.

Even though the constitutional progress of Malaya had been affected by the terrorist campaign waged by the local Communist Party from 1948 onwards, the Federation of Malaya duly attained full independence in August 1957, though only after a vigorous military campaign in which local and other Commonwealth forces participated. With the support of the local government, and with the enemy clearly identified as communist, firm military action was successful, though it did not escape Labour criticism in Britain. An independent Malaya, whose rubber and tin were vital strategic materials, emerged as a firm ally of Britain in the Far East.

So far the process of 'decolonisation', as it came to be known, appears as relatively smooth and orderly. Indeed subsequently many other dependencies were not so much to win independence, as to have it thrust upon them after scarcely a ripple of local agitation. The special problems of some of the territories, however, faced the British government with fierce political controversy at home and local violence and disorder, thus bringing out into the open some of the more painful aspects of the retreat from Empire. In this period, the Colonial Secretary occupied one of the hottest seats in the British Cabinet and the office enjoyed a political importance greater than at any time since the era of Joseph Chamberlain. To harassed officials and their political masters, under constant attack in Parliament and elsewhere from the increasingly vociferous anti-imperialist lobby in the British Labour Party, crisis appeared to follow crisis. The bipartisan approach to colonial policy which had characterised the 1940s broke down under a welter of Labour criticism of Lyttleton's 'insensitive' handling of colonial problems.

These problems were of bewildering diversity. In British Guiana, the 1953 elections, held under a new constitution which provided for a democratic franchise and a large measure of internal self-government, placed in office ministers of the People's Progress Party led by Dr Cheddi Jagan. Their conduct in office appeared to substantiate British official fears of communist influence – always a sensitive issue in the Americas. The ministers were dismissed, the constitution suspended, and troops and a cruiser were despatched to the capital, Georgetown. The left wing of the Labour party in

Britain protested at the fate of a democratically elected radical government, but in general the Labour leadership rejected what was seen as Jagan's attempt to set up a one-party state. It was not yet appreciated that the 'Westminster model' of parliamentary democracy would seldom flourish in tropical territories, and that the one-party state would soon typify political life in many of the non-white independent states of the Commonwealth.

The Conservative administration's difficulties with the left-wing Dr Jagan are perhaps easier to understand than the dispute with the Kabaka Mutesa II, hereditary ruler of Buganda in the Uganda protectorate. Buganda was an advanced 'native state' of the type so much admired by the exponents of indirect rule. The Kabaka, motivated in part by suspicions that the British might be planning to absorb Buganda into some future East African Federation, pressed for the separation of Buganda from the rest of the Protectorate and eventually denounced the Agreement of 1900 under which he was bound to accept British advice. In November 1953, he was sent into exile in London at the behest of the governor, Sir Andrew Cohen. Cohen was widely recognised as one of the most liberal and progressive administrators in the Colonial Office, but even he could not easily come to terms with the new nationalist spirit abroad in Africa – admittedly expressed in this case in the somewhat unlikely guise of a Cambridge-educated, traditional ruler who was an honorary captain in the Grenadier Guards.

The dilemmas of the last phase of Empire were most cruelly exposed in the crises concerning Cyprus, Kenya and central Africa. Cyprus may be taken first. Unlike most of the other problem territories, the island had a wholly European population, albeit divided into rival Greek and Turkish communities. There was no question, therefore, of the preparation of a backward people for self-government; what was in question was how a political formula could be worked out which would satisfy the aspirations of the Greeks, many of whom favoured *enosis* or union with Greece, and the Turks, who certainly preferred the continuation of British rule to *enosis*.

For the British government there was an overriding strategic consideration. Cyprus was a fortress colony, and the initial British position was expressed with an embarrassing lack of ambiguity by Henry Hopkinson, the Minister of State at the colonial office, when he told the House of Commons in 1954 that there would 'never' be a change of sovereignty in Cyprus:

There are certain territories in the Commonwealth which, owing to their particular circumstances can never expect to be fully independent. . . . The question of the abrogation of British sovereignty cannot arise.[3]

The strategic considerations appeared to be reinforced by the final withdrawal of British troops from the Suez Canal Zone in March 1956, although the Suez crisis subsequently exposed the limitations of Cyprus as a military base. The Greek Cypriots meanwhile had embarked on a major effort to achieve their objective of union with Greece. A political campaign was led with consummate skill by the Archbishop of Cyprus, Makarios III, while Colonel Grivas organised a guerrilla army, EOKA, to harry the British.

In 1956 Makarios was sent into a twelve-month exile in the Seychelles Islands, and the British mounted a major military campaign against EOKA. The latter, however, enjoyed a wide measure of sympathy among the Greek population and Field Marshal Harding was unable to repeat the success which Templer had achieved in dealing with the Malayan emergency. Moreover, the detention without trial and other emergency measures carried more than their usual burden of international political embarrassment when applied in a Mediterranean island with a population having strong ethnic links with two of Britain's NATO allies. The British government slowly backed down from Hopkinson's 'never'. Lord Salisbury, one of the last active Conservative politicians who adhered to the old imperial tradition, resigned in disgust when in 1957 the new Prime Minister, Harold Macmillan, released Archbishop Makarios.

Within two years Cyprus's right to full independence had been conceded, and Cyprus became a sovereign republic in 1960, guaranteed by Britain, Greece and Turkey. Britain retained certain 'sovereign base areas', perhaps out of respect for Hopkinson's earlier assertion, described by Colin Cross as 'the last full-blooded statement of imperial claim by an official British spokesman'.[4] Independence unfortunately did not end communal strife between Greek and Turk but, as first president of Cyprus, Britain's former *bête noir* Makarios soon established himself as a respected Commonwealth statesman. By 1974, however, the island had been partitioned as the result of a Turkish invasion which established a Turkish sector in the north. The British bases were unaffected by, and were apparently no deterrent to, this act of nationalist violence.

Even more remarkable than in the case of Makarios was the change in the British attitude to the Kenyan Jomo Kenyatta, a change which itself symbolises the evolution of colonial policy in the decade 1953–63. Pre-war Kenyan politics had been dominated by the European settlers who looked forward to the establishment of a 'white dominion' in east Africa. In 1946 Kenyatta had returned to Kenya from a long stay in England and set about organising African political opinion through the medium of his Kenya African Union. However, African grievances were not expressed only by 'constitutional' means. The Mau Mau, a secret society recruited from the largest tribe, the Kikuyu, began a guerrilla campaign involving attacks on European farms and the assassination of 'loyal' African leaders.

The end of 1952 saw the proclamation of a state of emergency and the arrival of British troops to fight the guerrillas. In the following year Kenyatta, suspected by the authorities of complicity in Mau Mau, was arrested and sentenced to seven years in prison. Colonial Secretary Lyttleton saw the African leader as 'a daemonic figure with extreme left-wing views'.[5] Yet almost exactly ten years after his conviction Kenyatta became Prime Minister of a Kenya on the verge of complete independence (December 1963). Subsequently the British found Kenyatta's regime one of the most congenial of those controlling the new independent states of Africa.

The triumph of African nationalism in Kenya had not been achieved simply by violence; the British were well able to contain Mau Mau and the state of emergency was ended in 1960. However, the effect of the Mau Mau crisis had brought 'the imperial factor' strongly back into Kenyan politics, and had ended the policy of drift whereby more and more power had devolved on the local settler community. In the last years of colonial rule, the decision-making power rested firmly with Whitehall where ministers and officials, particularly after the arrival at the Colonial Office in 1959 of the Tory radical Iain Macleod, came to accept the inevitability of rapid African political advance. Though there might be considerable resistance from some of the settlers, backed up by elements in the Conservative Party at home, the situation in Kenya was fundamentally different from that in Rhodesia where the settlers, granted responsible government in 1923, were able to carry their fight for political power into 1979. In Kenya, however, the troops, police and administration remained firmly under Whitehall control until the Africans achieved self-government. The transition was eased by various other factors. As George Bennett has put it: 'The chrysalis for the transformation from white to black power was provided by the idea of multi-racial partnership'.[6]

In pursuit of this principle, Kenya from 1954 onwards went through a bewildering series of constitutional changes. Finally, however, effective power passed to the black majority, and indeed many of the European settlers became reconciled to the change. They recognised in Kenyatta a man able to provide Kenya with a strong government which would end the uncertainties of the last years of colonial rule and provide a favourable climate for investment and expansion. Adjustments to the new Kenya would be difficult, but even the farmers of the former 'White Highlands' had the guarantee of a fair price for their land under a compensation scheme arranged with the British government.

Despite the bloodshed of the Mau Mau emergency, Kenya in the end proved one of the success stories of the retreat from Empire. The interests of local Europeans were adequately safeguarded and in the post-independence period Britain enjoyed cordial relations with the new government. In the other east African territories, where settlers were hardly a problem, the transition to independence had been notably smoother. In 1961 Tanganyika, which had always had rather special status first as a League of Nations Mandate and then as a United Nations Trust Territory, became independent. The next year Uganda became self-governing; there the problem had been the devising of constitutional arrangements which would reconcile pan-Ugandan nationalism, represented by Milton Obote, and Baganda particularism represented by the Kabaka (long since restored by the British).

In central Africa, however, the problem of decolonisation proved the most difficult of all, and indeed at one time looked insoluble in Southern Rhodesia. During the period 1953–65 there was no violence comparable to that in Kenya, Malaya or Cyprus, yet central Africa provided the climax to the retreat from Empire, a problem so daunting for Prime Minister Macmillan that eventually he provided his most senior colleague, R. A. Butler, with a Secretaryship of State devoted exclusively to it.

There were a number of reasons for the intensity of British concern about central Africa, not least being concern to maintain control of the region's natural resources. In 1960 the gross value of sales of Northern Rhodesian copper touched £132 million – such fruits of economic imperialism could not be lightly abandoned. The crux of the problem lay, however, with the largest community of white settlers in British colonial Africa. Until the end of the 1950s, successive British governments had pursued policies reasonably congenial to the local Europeans, and, to a much greater extent than in Kenya, had allowed effective power to pass into the hands of those Europeans. When the British government therefore wished to trim their sails to the 'wind of change' and force concessions to African nationalist demands, they found a settler political leadership willing and able to offer fierce resistance. Moreover, that resistance received strong support from the right wing of the Conservative Party, which bitterly resented what they regarded as a sell-out to communist-inspired African nationalist agitators.

When the Conservatives assumed office in 1951, they had enthusiastically endorsed plans for a federation of the three central African territories – the self-governing (i.e. by the European minority) colony of Southern Rhodesia, and the two protectorates of Northern Rhodesia and Nyasaland. The economic case for federation was considered to be overwhelming: Southern Rhodesia had a sophisticated industrial base whereas Northern Rhodesia had the huge and valuable natural resource of its copper deposits. Federation would attract investment, particularly for huge public works projects such as the Kariba Dam on the Zambesi. There were political advantages too – it was hoped that the federation would develop into a new great independent Dominion – independent but 'British' in sentiment, a counterpoise to the Union of South Africa which since 1948 had become progressively more dominated by Afrikaner nationalism. As far as the African majority were concerned, they would, arguably, benefit economically from partnership with the Europeans. It was even claimed by apologists that some of the cruder aspects of racial discrimination would disappear in due course. Nonetheless Africans were envisaged initially as very much the junior partners in the federal experiment – the partnership between European and African, as one European leader put it with striking candour, would be one of the rider and the horse.

The Federation of Rhodesia and Nyasaland thus came into existence in 1953 as one of the last efforts at creative statesmanship within a distinctly imperial framework, reminiscent of the drastic administrative reorganisations in the latter days of the Roman Empire. The federation lasted just over ten years. From the start, it was fiercely opposed by the Africans of Northern Rhodesia who saw it as a backdoor method of settler rule. Awareness of African opposition and suspicion of settler motives had caused the British Labour Party to withdraw their earlier support for the scheme, and the federal controversy was one of the major contributory factors in the breakdown of the bipartisan colonial policy at Westminster.

The constitutional arrangements were indeed cumbersome. A federal executive and legislature were created with powers in such matters as taxation, communications and defence. The executive and legislature were effectively controlled by the local Europeans, but the Federation was not granted full independence, and within the federal structure Southern Rhodesia retained the self-government enjoyed since 1923 and the protectorates of Northern Rhodesia and Nyasaland remained a Colonial Office responsibility. The stresses in the structure were evident from the beginning; Africans and some officials in the protectorates resented the 'imposition' of federation, whereas the local European leadership wished to advance quickly to Dominion status, i.e. full independence, despite the narrowness of the franchise which placed only 67,039 voters on the electoral roll for the first Federal general election.

Until the end of 1959 the British government remained firmly committed to the Federal experiment, despite increasing evidence of African unrest in central Africa. Particularly serious were events in Nyasaland where a well-organised nationalist movement led by Dr Hastings Banda, a former London medical practitioner, had led to the proclamation of a state of emergency by the governor and what the Devlin Commission described as a 'police state'.[7] Coming on top of the Hola Camp incident in Kenya, when eleven Mau Mau detainees died as a result of ill-treatment by camp officials, the Devlin Report called into question the whole basis of British colonial policy. There were also disturbances in Northern and Southern Rhodesia, though events in the latter territory were outside the control of the Colonial Office. The British general election of 1959 however, though it confirmed the Macmillan government in power, led to a turning point in colonial policy. Macmillan and his new Colonial Secretary, Iain Macleod, became convinced that the tempo of African advance must be quickened, and that the nettle of decolonisation must be grasped in territories like Kenya and Northern Rhodesia, where settlers had aspired to political power.

In central Africa the issue was basically simple. If African nationalists gained power through constitutional change in Northern Rhodesia and Nyasaland, those two territories would secede and the Federation would break up. The crisis, however, was not to be resolved without a fierce struggle between the British government and Roy Welensky, the Federal Prime Minister. Welensky, the son of a poor white eastern European immigrant, ex-boxer, railwayman and trade union leader, was a tough, determined and resourceful politician who was able to give the urbane Macmillan some hard knocks before eventually going down to defeat. Although the Federal government possessed considerable military forces, including a powerful airforce, Welensky, unlike Ian Smith in 1965, did not push his resistance to the open rebellion which Macmillan at one point feared.[8]

Macmillan's attitude was made clear during his famous 'wind of change' tour of Africa in 1960. In October of that year, the Monckton Commission reported that 'the strength of African opposition in the northern territories is such that Federation cannot . . . be maintained in its present form'.[9] In 1961 and 1962 respectively Nyasaland and Northern Rhodesia obtained new constitutions which placed African nationalist ministers in office, though not without, in Northern Rhodesia, a desperate wrangle over the absurdly complex franchise provisions of the new scheme. Eventually the right of both territories to secede from the Federation was admitted, and the ill-starred experiment came to an end in December 1963. The independence of Nyasaland (as Malawi) and Northern Rhodesia (as Zambia) duly followed in 1964.

These events in relation to central Africa have been recounted in some detail because, in effect, they closed a major chapter in the book of Britain's imperial history. Despite the pressures of world opinion, local settlers and African nationalists, Macmillan and his ministers were still able to a very large extent to determine the pace of events, and to act decisively in defeating settler ambitions outside Southern Rhodesia. The quickening of the pace of change was the most remarkable aspect of Britain's Africa policy from 1959 onwards. Thus Nigeria, which had made steady constitutional progress since the end of the Second World War, only attained independence in 1960; Tanganyika, which had been regarded in the late 1950s as still a decade away from independence, reached it in 1961. It was no longer a question of the viability of a territory either economically as a national unit, or of its 'readiness' for self-government.[10] In 1964, after all, the new state of Zambia had only 100 university graduates and 1000 secondary school graduates out of an African population of five million. 'All that mattered was that an indigenous political élite, with some degree of local support, should exist and be willing to take over' – thus avoiding the bloody chaos of the Congo after the abrupt Belgian withdrawal in 1960.[11]

By 1966 independence had come to all the territories for which the Colonial Office had been responsible in Africa, and to the larger West Indian colonies. One piece of unfinished African business remained, however, to provide successive British governments with an unwelcome hangover from the imperial age. The dissolution of the Central African Federation left intact the constitutional position of the self-governing colony of Southern Rhodesia, over which Whitehall had never exercised direct administrative control. A new constitution had been introduced in 1961 which gave some very limited political opportunities to Africans, but had been boycotted by the nationalist movements. The white-settler regime was determined to retain power in European hands for an indefinite period, but at the same time wished to emulate the African nationalist regimes to the north in the achievement of complete independence from Britain. No agreement could be reached with the Labour government which came to power in Britain in October 1964 – indeed both the Labour and Conservative leadership were convinced that it would be wholly inconsistent with British policy towards the other African territories to permit Southern Rhodesia to proceed to independence under constitutional arrangements which did not provide effective guarantees for eventual 'majority rule'. Subsequently, after Harold Wilson, the British Prime Minister, had rather unwisely made it clear that force would not be used against the settlers, the Southern Rhodesian government rebelled in November 1965, making a unilateral declaration of independence.

The 'rebellion' was a strange affair. Although the Governor and at first the judiciary remained loyal, the Governor's instructions to the armed forces and police permitted them to carry on with their 'normal' duties, thus in effect sustaining the rebellion. Although the Rhodesians had inherited the military hardware (including the airforce) from the Federal armed forces, they could hardly have withstood British armed intervention, which Macmillan appears to have contemplated during the crisis with Welensky.[12]

The British chose instead to fight by invoking the aid of the United Nations in the imposition of economic sanctions, but the rebellion did not collapse rapidly, as Harold Wilson had rashly prophesied. The final chapter of the history of the colonial Empire in Africa thus involved painful humiliations for Britain, earning her from one prominent Zambian the description of 'toothless bulldog'. It was ironic that the only rebellion which actually ousted British constitutional authority during the retreat from Empire was by those very European settlers who had, in that period, protested fervent loyalty to the British Crown, and from whose ranks had come Roy Welensky, the last statesman to be sustained by Rhodes' imperial vision.

There was destined to be a further irony. As we shall see, in 1979 the rebellion finally came to an end and British colonial rule was established for a brief transitional period prior to legal independence.[13] The principal agency which brought about this transformation, however, was the armed struggle of the black nationalists whose counterparts in other territories had once appeared as the enemies of British imperialism during the independence struggle.

## THE NEW COMMONWEALTH IN THE MAKING

As Britain's colonies became independent, the Commonwealth saw its membership strikingly increased. The 'Old Dominions' were reduced to a paltry numerical minority, jostled by new 'Commonwealth Club' members with black, brown and yellow skins. Moreover the old 'white' guard was reduced by a quarter in 1961 when Dr Verwoed's South Africa, about to become a republic, applied for continuing membership of the Commonwealth, after the sloughing off of Dominion status, and withdrew the application when it was clear that it would be refused due to the opposition of largely 'new Commonwealth' members who naturally abhorred *apartheid*.[14]

It was, from the outset, arguable whether this drastically enlarged Commonwealth had much common purpose or, indeed, many common interests. Its members, for the most part, were not kith and kin of the 'mother country', and sometimes took the opportunity publicly to attack aspects of British policy. Nor was there necessarily any love lost between neighbouring Commonwealth countries, as several Indo-Pakistan conflicts, East African border tensions, the secession of Singapore from the federation of

Malaysia, and the disintegration of the West Indies federation were painfully to show.

Increasingly, Commonwealth Conferences were as marked by bitter fratricidal strife as by harmony, with Britain's vote often no more powerful or persuasive than that of any member – even the newest or most backward. The fitful export over so many years of British democratic principles had come home to roost with a vengeance. Indeed the day was not far off when it could be suggested that Britain should be expelled from the Commonwealth Club if her alleged transgressions sufficiently offended the majority of fellow members.

Yet the fact that so many ex-colonies had chosen to join the 'new Commonwealth' persuaded some latter-day imperialists in Britain that the days of Britain's imperial power were being miraculously extended into the era of decolonisation. Leopold Amery, once one of the Milner 'kindergarten' and a Colonial and Dominions Secretary of State between the wars, wrote in 1953: ' . . . other nations now outside [the Commonwealth] may well decide to join it in course of time. . . . Who knows but what [sic] it may become a nucleus round which a future world order will crystallise?'[15] Although others subscribed to this optimism (Beaverbrook's *Daily Express* even suggested Israel and Norway as potential members of the Commonwealth), Amery's hopes were in effect so much pie in the sky.

Still, there were bonds to be cherished, and even extended. Imperial trading preferences encouraged inter-Commonwealth commerce – and Joseph Chamberlain had come to believe half a century before that this connection was likely to prove the most fruitful. Commonwealth citizens also had the right to enter Britain and to settle there; were, in fact, British citizens in the sense of Palmerston's famous 'civis Romanus sum' speech during the Don Pacifico debate in 1850.[16] By the early 1960s tens of thousands of West Indians, Indians, Pakistanis, and others had emigrated to Britain's booming industrial towns.

This flood of immigrants aroused hostility in some sections of British society, and the 1962 Commonwealth Immigrants Act and the further tightening in 1965 of the number of work permits issued, reduced the influx and at the same time showed the hollowness of any ideal of a common Commonwealth nationality. The restrictions on immigration imposed by Britain were all the more shabby since Republic of Ireland immigrants were allowed free access to what was technically a foreign state, and even foreigners, though they still had to obtain work permits, were not subjected to numerical restrictions. Ironically, those Britons on the political right, while tempted at one stage to put high hopes on to the new Commonwealth, were also often the most strident opponents of unrestricted immigration.

Was it all a question of colour prejudice? Sir Grantly Adams, the West Indian federal statesman, asked innocently, 'Can a coloured population of less than one per cent destroy this great country?'[17] Some of the British electorate certainly seemed to have feared so, and the general election of 1964 was marked by some unscrupulous campaigning on the subject – most controversially in Smethwick, where a safe Labour majority in a constituency with a large number of coloured immigrants was overturned, against the national 'swing', by a Tory candidate not averse to exploiting racial fears.

This was hardly the stuff of a new, purified and truly international Commonwealth spirit. Nor were Labour governments inevitably more liberal than Conservative administrations on the issue of 'new Commonwealth' immigration. When Kenya had achieved independence in 1963, the 180,000 Asians living there had been allowed the right to retain British citizenship. When, a year later, Asians found themselves under pressure to leave from a Kenyatta government which chose to regard them as foreigners, Wilson's Labour administration hastily imposed an annual quota of 1500 on Kenyan Asians wishing to enter Britain. These were indeed muddied waters.

In fact, by the early 1960s the complacency of many post-war supporters of the new Commonwealth had been rudely shattered. Shortly after the war, the British Labour Minister, John Strachey, was able to say of the Commonwealth 'to know a no-ball from a googly and a point of order from a supplementary question is genuinely to have something in common'. By 1965, however, a love of cricket seemed one of the few imperial legacies destined to survive a host of intractable political and economic threats to Commonwealth unity.

Not the least of these threats was Britain's application to join the European Economic Community. Membership of the Common Market was incompatible with a continuing system of imperial preferential tariffs. If, moreover, the EEC was to develop, as many of its supporters hoped, into a sort of United States of Europe, this would have the effect of lessening Britain's ability, or desire, to work closely within the Commonwealth. Though the Labour Party, on the whole, and the Conservatives, in part, had misgivings over the potential benefits of Britain's membership of the Common Market, the Macmillan government made the first serious overture to the EEC in 1962.[18] This approach was dealt a humiliating rebuff by President de Gaulle of France, who, obsessed with the notion of 'Anglo-Saxons' rather than 'Reds' under the Common Market bed, said, in effect, 'No'. Still, a precedent had been set, and after Labour's victory in the 1964 general election, the new Prime Minister, Harold Wilson, was to edge cautiously towards renewing Britain's application for membership of the European Economic Community. In the long term, imperial preference was doomed.

Moreover, the Commonwealth was no longer, if it ever had been, a diplomatic unity. The growing black and brown majority within the organisation saw to that. Some newly independent Commonwealth countries, of which India was the most powerful, declared themselves to be 'non-aligned' in the polarisation resulting from the 'Cold War'. At the same time, it was difficult to believe that these non-aligned nations were not, in the last resort, in the western camp – as in the case of India after her frontier conflicts with the People's Republic of China in the 1960s. The Suez invasion of 1956, however, had been demonstrably not the last resort, and the new Commonwealth members identified with Egypt rather than with Britain during this unhappy episode; Canada, too, was anxious to disassociate herself from Anglo-French aggression, though predictably Australia and New Zealand offered their support to the mother country.[19]

What, indeed, could the Commonwealth agree on in diplomatic terms? One, more or less, unifying theme was dislike of South Africa's system of *apartheid*. In 1961 the newly created South African Republic was, in effect, prevented from remaining within the Commonwealth Club after the overwhelming majority of members had expressed their hostility to such racial discrimination. Anti-*apartheid* feeling, however, gave the Commonwealth no more than a fitful experience of common purpose. Perhaps one mutually acceptable principle of Commonwealth membership might have been found in the promotion of peace within the organisation. The Indo-Pakistan war of 1965 destroyed that principle, and subsequent tensions between member states have not been confined to the Indian subcontinent. In the same year, Britain's handling of Southern Rhodesia's unilateral declaration of independence put a severe strain on mutual Commonwealth goodwill – Tanzania even leaving the organisation for a time in disgust.

Paradoxically, as events in 1965 demonstrated the fragility of Commonwealth unity, the first piece of formal machinery for promoting that unity was set up. This was the Commonwealth Secretariat, a sort of civil service designed to up-date and co-ordinate information among members. Although the need for such a secretariat had long been evident, some Commonwealth Prime Ministers cherished the informal qualities of their meetings – 'the talk round a table between friends' as Clement Attlee put it. When the secretariat was created, the Prime Ministers agreed that its staff and duties would 'expand pragmatically in the light of experience, subject always to the approval of governments'. A Canadian, Arnold Smith, was the new organisation's first Secretary-General, with a multiracial staff to support him.

In 1965 the conference of Prime Ministers also approved a Commonwealth Foundation, to develop links between professional bodies within the organisation. Other formal associations included the Commonwealth Agricultural Bureau, the Education Liaison Committee and the Economic Consultative Council. As with the Commonwealth itself, however, these various organisations were essentially voluntary and lacking any executive power: persuasion was their means and mutual co-operation their end.

When it was suggested that a Commonwealth Supreme Court should be established as a final court of appeal, the proposal was decisively rebuffed. The Judicial Committee of the Privy Council in Britain still served that function – though only for those countries that chose to use it. It was very much in keeping with the Commonwealth principle of freedom of association that this should have happened. A common devotion to freedom of association, to voluntary co-operation, to a loose organisation were fundamental to the Commonwealth as it had evolved by 1965 – indeed, though narrowly representative, Southern Rhodesia's declaration of independence in the same year was, in some ways, in keeping with these principles. Whether the Commonwealth could, however, actually make something more concrete out of its benign and voluntary structure was difficult to predict.

# Part 6

# CRISIS IN CONFIDENCE, 1966–71

The period from 1966–71 was not a happy one for the Commonwealth. Several member states experienced military coups or civil wars. The white Rhodesian rebellion was not quelled, and some African countries showed their disillusionment with Britain's failure to solve the crisis by breaking off diplomatic relations. Singapore left the Malaysian federation. Britain herself faced increasingly serious internal disturbances in Northern Ireland, and provoked bitter criticism from other Commonwealth members for her continuing strict control of coloured immigration and for acts of alleged partiality towards the white supremacists of southern Africa. It was also clear that Britain was determined to join the European Economic Community, and the surprise Conservative victory in the 1970 General Election put the enthusiastic pro-marketeer Edward Heath into 10 Downing Street.[1] To many observers the new Commonwealth seemed to have lost any real sense of purpose or cohesion, and to be drifting towards an acrimonious and inevitable dissolution.

At first, however, the signs were relatively promising. The British government, led by Harold Wilson, seemed well-disposed towards the Commonwealth. Wilson had not yet revealed himself as pro-Common Market. On the contrary, the early years of his premiership were marked by an almost unfashionable enthusiasm for the Commonwealth. He appeared to take it seriously as a world force – as his proposal in 1965 to set up a Commonwealth peace mission to help end the Vietnamese war was to prove. When the Anguilla crisis occurred in 1969 it was Wilson's government that acted with Palmerstonian zest, sending in British troops to keep the peace on this tiny Caribbean island.[2]

Wilson also made a brisk start to his handling of Rhodesia's unilateral declaration of independence. Although he rather hastily ruled out the use of force, Wilson made RAF planes available for the protection of Rhodesia's northern neighbour Zambia, and entered into an economic sanctions war with Ian Smith's illegal regime in Salisbury. At a special Commonwealth Conference held in Lagos early in 1966, the British Prime Minister managed to persuade most of the African delegations that he meant business over Rhodesia and that sanctions had a good chance of working.

He was not, however, without his critics. The fact that the first batch of sanctions imposed against Rhodesia did not include oil confirmed the suspicions of some states that Britain would soon seek a compromise settlement with the rebel government. Wilson's two dramatic, and nearly successful, negotiations with Ian Smith aboard HMS *Tiger* and later the *Fearless* were seen by many as confirmation that Britain was preparing for a sell-out of black interests under a smoke-screen of a complex and baffling restructuring of the Rhodesian constitution.[3] Tanzania and Ghana had already, in December 1965, broken off diplomatic relations in protest at Britain's inactivity.

In 1966 the Canadian Prime Minister and elder statesman Lester Pearson had said:

> The idea that a white minority regime might attain and retain independence on a minority racial basis – this is contrary not only to democratic principles and basic human rights but it violates the multi-racial character of our Commonwealth and could destroy our association.[4]

By 1971 it did seem as if the failure to bring down the Smith regime could destroy the Commonwealth. Tanzania and Zambia were driven into closer contact with communist China. Indeed the communist powers were able to make much political capital out of the apparently half-hearted way in which many capitalist countries applied sanctions against Rhodesia.

Discontent at Britain's arguably ambivalent attitude towards the white minority regimes of southern Africa was expressed clearly at home at the end of the decade. Anti-*apartheid* demonstrations disturbed the South African rugby team's tour of the United Kingdom in 1969–70, and a Stop-the-70-Tour Committee was formed to protest at the scheduled visit of South Africa's cricketers. Although the 1970 cricket tour was eventually banned, the newly elected Conservative government, led by Edward Heath, provoked angry Commonwealth reaction by announcing that the sale of arms to South Africa would be resumed. To many new Commonwealth statesmen it seemed incomprehensible that the British government should so blatantly antagonise African, and indeed world, opinion, for the sake of maintaining Britain's trading and strategic links with South Africa. How much trade with Black Africa was lost as a consequence is difficult to calculate. As for the continuing use of the Simonstown naval base, its value rested on the assumption, then somewhat insubstantial, of a confrontation with Russia in the Indian Ocean.

The accession of Edward Heath to the British premiership carried one further threat to the fragile flower of Commonwealth unity. Heath was a dedicated advocate of Britain joining the European Economic Community. If sufficiently favourable terms of entry could be negotiated, there was little doubt that the Conservative government, despite the vehement opposition of some right-wingers like Enoch Powell, would force Britain into the Common Market. The full implications of that move were disturbing both to the old Dominions and to the non-European members of the Commonwealth. In fact, it seemed to many observers that for Britain to join the EEC meant turning her back on the Commonwealth. It was an odd posture for the mother country to assume, and caused New Zealand's Prime Minister Keith Holyoake to remark: 'We are fighting for our livelihood'.

Further afield, Commonwealth countries endured traumas of a more abrupt nature. In 1966 Kwame Nkrumah was deposed by an army coup which occurred while he was on a Vietnam peace mission to China. The new government, calling itself the National Liberation Council, led by Major-General Joseph Ankrah, released many of Nkrumah's political prisoners. The ex-president's supporters melted away like snow under the Ghanaian sun, and Nkrumah was forced to find refuge in Guinea. The 'Founder of the Nation' was now denounced as a corrupt dictator who had lined his own pocket. Despite doubts as to the army's true intentions, a new constitution was framed, and in 1969 a general election marked Ghana's return to a western-style democracy under a civilian government led by Kofi Busia. It was an encouraging opportunity to start again.[5]

In 1966 the other great West African Commonwealth country, Nigeria, lurched towards civil war. The Government headed by the northerner Sir Abubakar Tafawa Balewa was overthrown by a military coup led by officers drawn chiefly from the Ibo tribe. The incident was an indication of the power of tribal animosities between the Ibos of eastern Nigeria, the Hausas of the north, and the Yoruba of the west. After much bloodshed and confusion, the Ibo people sought safety in their own state of Biafra, led by the charismatic Colonel Ojukwu. The leader of the now fragmented federation, Colonel Gowon, was determined to crush Biafra's secession.

The ensuing civil war provided the rest of the world with the unedifying spectacle of Biafra being slowly strangled to death by encircling Nigerian forces. Apart from the losses suffered on both sides in the bitter fighting, Biafrans had to face the horrors of mass starvation and disease. Attempts by international bodies such as the Red Cross to provide aid were often thwarted by diplomatic wrangles and red tape. Early in 1970 the war was at last over: Ojukwu flew into exile, and Nigeria set about salvaging the principle of national unity from the ruins of Biafra.[6] Slowly, thanks mostly to the federal government's good sense, the nation's wounds were bound up and Ibos gradually returned to employment in other parts of the country. The divisive spectre of tribal antipathies had not, however, been exorcised for the rest of Africa.

In Kenya, tribal divisions were compounded by the presence of influential European and Asian minorities in the population. Although Jomo Kenyatta and most of his ministers came from the Kikuyu tribe, which had provided the driving force behind the Mau Mau uprising, the obvious heir apparent to Kenyatta's position was the brilliant Tom Mboya – who was from the Luo people. Tribal antagonism, however, made it unlikely that Mboya would reach the highest office in the land, and in 1969 he was murdered as he walked out of a Nairobi chemist's shop. Luo tribesmen went on the rampage in Nairobi, even stoning Kenyatta himself in their outrage. A Kikuyu, Isaac Njorage, was eventually hanged for Mboya's murder, but this act of justice could not eliminate inter-tribal tensions.[7]

In Zambia, President Kaunda's government had to keep the confidence of over seventy tribes. Anxious to avoid fuelling the fires of tribalism, Kaunda was driven to ban political parties based simply upon tribal allegiances. Kaunda's own party, however, the United National Independence Party, was itself torn by tribal rivalries. When Simon Kapwepwe, Kaunda's long-standing friend and associate, seemed to be aspiring to lead the pro-Bemba faction in the UNIP, the president refused to allow him to resign the Vice-Presidency – thus hoping to keep him from playing a dangerous tribal role. In 1969 Kaunda took the drastic step of assuming the major functions of government himself. This was not the move of a megalomaniac. On the contrary, Kenneth Kaunda's obvious integrity and strength of character seemed the essential cement without which Zambia's social, political and economic structure would disintegrate. One-man rule, however, no matter how benevolent, was still a long way away from the old ideal of Westminster-style parliamentary government.[8]

As if the internal tribal problems of various African Commonwealth countries were not enough to contend with, economic and political pressures produced a variety of responses – not all of them welcomed in the west. Britain's failure to bring down the white supremacist government in Rhodesia, and the continuing pattern of *apartheid* and oppression in South Africa, made some African states look towards the communist world for support. By 1971, there were Chinese advisers and technicians in Tanzania, and the Peking government had built the 'friendship' textile mill. An interest-free Chinese loan was enabling Tanzania and Zambia to build the 'Tan-Zam' railway line to give Zambian copper access to the sea through territory other than Rhodesian and Portuguese. Though Russia's invasion of Czechoslovakia in 1968 disillusioned many African socialist leaders, African students still went to both the Soviet Union and China for further education and training. In practice, African states wanted to avoid communist domination as much as western interference in their domestic affairs. Still, the 1960s was a time of anxiety for western observers and governments; the non-aligned nations of Africa seemed to be engaged in a perilous flirtation with the major communist powers.[9]

Partly to counter communist influence, the 'old' members of the Commonwealth – Britain, Canada, Australia and New Zealand – gave as generously as they could to the Commonwealth Development Corporation which gave financial assistance to African members through the Special Commonwealth African Assistance Plan first established in 1960. By the mid-1960s India and Pakistan were making contributions on a modest scale, as were some of the African states themselves – the Gambia received aid from Ghana, for instance, and Tanzania from Nigeria.

Assistance took two main forms. One was capital, mostly loaned at low rates of interest or as a gift. Such capital went to establish new industries or to improve public services. In 1966, for example, African Commonwealth countries received £69,000,000 in aid from Britain and £5,000,000 from fellow-members of the organisation. The second form of assistance was in the provision of expert help and in the education of African students. By the mid-1960s Britain took about 1500 African students on special scholarships, while another 15,000 came after making their own financial arrangements. Help was also given in establishing institutions of higher education in African countries.

Aid, of course, was not simply an expression of western humanitarianism, though it was partly that. Aid was also intended to stabilise the economies and hence the political structures of newly independent states. Moreover, by helping African economies to develop, the west could look forward to a profitable growth in trade. In other words, aid was a covert form of investment – for both western and communist states. In a real sense, there was no such thing as 'aid without strings attached'.

By the mid-1960s Britain's trade with African Commonwealth states was a comparatively small proportion of her overall trade. Even Nigeria, the most important of Britain's African trading partners, contributed less than 1 per cent to Britain's trade. Apart from Nigeria, Zambia had her valuable copper exports, but countries like Kenya and Tanzania had a harder struggle to sell their agricultural products in a world market that was often oversupplied. As their economies developed, however, African states urgently needed machinery and manufactured goods, which could often only be paid for if the exporting nations gave them assistance. Commonwealth aid schemes help to explain the dependence of countries like Malawi, Uganda and Tanzania upon trade within the organisation. In 1967, for example, Malawi made 70 per cent of its purchases within the Commonwealth, Uganda 60 per cent, and Tanzania 52 per cent.[10] The Commonwealth, with its preferential tariff scheme, also provided a valuable market for such states.

Further east the federation of Malaysia came into existence in 1963. It comprised Malaya, led by Tunku Abdul Rahman, the island entrepot of Singapore, and the British colonies in North Borneo, Sarawak and Sabah. Only Brunei, the tiny neighbour of Sarawak and Sabah, refused to join the federation, hoping to achieve commercial success through its oil revenues.

Malaysia was soon beset by troubles. President Sukarno, of

Indonesia, coveting North Borneo, resented the inclusion of Sarawak and Sabah in the federation. A small-scale guerrilla campaign ensued and even included an Indonesian paratroop raid on Malaya itself. The Commonwealth rallied to Malaysia's cause, and Britain, Australia and New Zealand sent troops to help the Malaysians; Canada gave less direct military assistance.

Although Indonesian hostility was contained, the federation suffered a self-inflicted wound when Singapore, led by the able Lee Kuan Yew, seceded from the organisation in 1965. Both Singapore and Malaysia prospered in the aftermath of this move, although Singapore favoured free trade and Malaysia imposed protective tariffs. Social reform in Malaysia had produced a 75 per cent literacy rate by 1970, and important agricultural and industrial development had taken place.

However, racial tensions, primarily between Malays and Chinese, continued to trouble both Malaysia and Singapore. Although in Singapore the Malay minority seemed relatively reconciled to the dominance of the Chinese majority, Malaysia suffered from severe racial rioting in 1969, and in May of that year parliamentary democracy was temporarily suspended. Both Malaysia and Singapore, moreover, feared communist expansion in South-East Asia, and were relieved in 1970 by the commitment of the newly elected Conservative government of Edward Heath to maintain a modest British military presence in the area. Although Tunku Abdul Rahman retired in 1970, Malaysia and Singapore had come of age as Commonwealth countries by the end of the decade – indeed Malaysia began to give aid to other emerging member states, particularly in Africa.[11]

Elsewhere, a whole crop of small territories achieved independence: British Guiana in 1966, Mauritius in 1968, Fiji and Tonga in 1970, the Federation of Arab Emirates (in the Persian Gulf) in 1971, Southern Yemen (including the troublesome ex-protectorate of Aden) in 1967. Although Britain still ruled colonies like Hong Kong, St Helena, the Seychelles, St Vincent and a number of similar territories, the Empire had effectively disintegrated by 1971. What was left was an organisation, the Commonwealth, of almost bewildering variety, yet lacking any truly cohesive force to bind it together. Whether it could survive the 1970s in any useful or recognisable form was plainly open to doubt.

# PART 7

# THE COMMONWEALTH
# REVIVED, 1971–80

As the Commonwealth Heads of Government assembled for their meeting in Singapore in January 1971, there were plenty of reasons for doubting the ability of the Commonwealth association to survive the decade in any real sense. As we have seen, the 1960s, despite the crises of decolonisation in Africa and elsewhere, had opened with bright hopes of a new Commonwealth spirit of international co-operation – the product of the free association of so many formerly subject peoples. Having shrugged off the imperial hangover, the Commonwealth could set an example to the world in functional co-operation between diverse countries and in the application of democratic principles of government.[1]

Such hopes had hardly been sustained through a period which had seen war between two Commonwealth states – India and Pakistan – a military coup followed by civil war in Nigeria, civil war in Cyprus, and military take-overs in Ghana and Sierra Leone. Britain's failure to deal effectively with Ian Smith's rebellion in Southern Rhodesia also provided a major and continuing threat to the survival of the Commonwealth from 1965 onwards. Dissatisfaction with Britain's policy on this issue led to the breaking off of diplomatic relations by Ghana and Tanzania, and to bitter wrangles at a succession of Commonwealth Conferences. Although the latter appeared to some commentators to serve no constructive purpose except as a forum for baiting the 'toothless British bulldog' at least the meetings offered some relief to African frustrations. Looking back on the 1960s, Lord Garner, Permanent Under-Secretary of State in the British Commonwealth Office until 1968, felt it was enough to claim, with the Abbe Siéyès, 'I survived'.[2]

In some respects, the balance sheet for the Commonwealth in the 1970s appeared little brighter. The decade opened with a rather bad-tempered Heads of Government meeting in Singapore in

January 1971, the first regular meeting to be held outside London. The new British Prime Minister, Edward Heath, committed to Europe and impatient with the relics of Empire, did not take kindly to the by now almost traditional attacks on Britain's Rhodesia policy, or to criticism of the renewal of British arms supplies to South Africa. The meeting unanimously endorsed a Declaration of Commonwealth Principles affirming the inalienable right of all citizens to 'participate by means of free and democratic political processes in framing the society in which they live'. However, not only the citizens of Rhodesia were denied this right. During the Singapore meeting, the President of Uganda, Dr Milton Obote, who had himself assumed presidential power by unconstitutional means in 1966, was ousted in a military coup led by General Idi Amin.

Thus the Singapore meeting, from which the ringing declaration of principles had emerged, was fated to coincide with the establishment in Uganda of a regime destined to become one of the most brutal dictatorships of the post-war era. The situation in Uganda posed an increasingly difficult problem for the Commonwealth. On the one hand, the principle of non-interference in each other's internal affairs appeared central to the Commonwealth partnership. There was also a reluctance to contemplate the novel step of expelling a member state because of the malpractice of a regime, which, it was hoped, would not survive for long. On the other hand, as evidence mounted of the excesses of the Amin regime, it proved difficult for the Commonwealth to remain silent.

Eventually, Amin (who once proposed that the headship of the Commonwealth should be made elective and offered himself as a candidate) caused consternation by threatening to attend the 'Jubilee' meeting of Heads of Government in London in 1977. In the absence of Amin and of any Ugandan representative, the Heads of Government publicly condemned in strong and unequivocal terms the 'massive violation of basic human rights in Uganda'[3]. As a group, however, the Commonwealth had no weapons other than words. The following year, Amin, conscious of mounting opposition from his own people to his rule, overreached himself by attempting an invasion of Uganda's Commonwealth neighbour Tanzania in order to occupy a disputed border area. The Tanzanians, aided by Ugandan exiles, responded with a full-scale invasion of Uganda. Kampala, the country's capital, was captured in April 1979, and Amin was driven into exile. His rule had devastated Uganda and left his successors an appalling task of political, economic and social reconstruction; it had also again produced the discomforting spectacle of war between fellow Commonwealth members. However, Ugandans ended the decade with the prospect of the first elections since independence in 1962. These elections duly took place in December 1980, and amidst some confusion, returned Milton Obote to power.

Apart from Uganda, other Commonwealth African countries were experiencing a difficult decade. Zambia, although remaining politically stable under President Kaunda's leadership, suffered from acute economic problems as a result of difficulties not of her own making. The continuation of the rebellion in Rhodesia until 1979 coupled with a slump in the price of copper (on which Zambia depended almost totally for export earnings) sadly impeded the country's development. In 1972, Zambia followed the Tanzanian example and the constitution was amended to provide for a one-party state. Kenya had also become a *de facto* one-party state in 1969 when the sole opposition party, the Kenya People's Union, was banned. The absence of a legal political opposition in Kenya, Tanzania, Zambia and Malawi, and, from 1978, in Sierra Leone, has led some unsympathetic commentators in Britain to refer to one-party 'dictatorships'.

None of those countries, however, had at any stage after independence an effective opposition party with a serious prospect of defeating the governing party at the polls. The one-party system, therefore, merely reflects the political realities and, paradoxically, increases the freedom of choice of the electorate who may unseat a cabinet minister in favour of another member of the governing party. By and large, the human rights record of these Commonwealth countries has been reasonably good and other democratic safeguards such as the independence of the judiciary have been preserved. The political stability enjoyed by the four countries has certainly been remarkable. In 1980, Presidents Banda of Malawi, Nyerere of Tanzania, and Kaunda of Zambia had all been in office since 1964, as had President Kenyatta of Kenya until his death in 1978, when he was succeeded peacefully, in accordance with the electoral procedures prescribed by the constitution, by the former Vice-President, Daniel arap Moi.

One casualty of the decade was the East African Community. This highly sophisticated mechanism of regional economic co-operation providing common railways, airways and currency systems for Tanzania, Uganda and Zambia foundered on the impossibility of collaboration with the Amin regime and on quarrels between Tanzania and Kenya. Although of course the Community was not a 'Commonwealth' organisation, it was an imperial relic of sorts, and it was sad to see the collapse of such a promising example of co-operation between three neighbouring Commonwealth states.

In West Africa, political developments in the two big Commonwealth states, Ghana and Nigeria, illustrated the difficulties a number of Commonwealth countries have experienced in the post-independence generation in developing an institutional framework for stable political life and for 'good government'.

Successive political crises in Ghana during the decade reflected the impact of economic difficulties, particularly the persistent inflationary pressures and unstable commodity prices which plagued so many third-world countries. In 1969, Ghana had returned to civilian constitutional government after the period of military rule which followed the overthrow of President Nkrumah in 1966. The experiment in multiparty democracy under a 'Westminster'-type constitution was destined to be short-lived. The civilian government under Dr Busia was widely blamed for economic mismanagement, and the military returned to power by another coup in 1972.

A second period of military rule did little to solve Ghana's economic problems. Resentment against the corruption of the higher echelon of the ruling junta led to a further spectacular coup by junior ranks in the armed forces in June 1979, shortly before civilian government was due to be re-established. The coup, led by the colourful figure of Flight-lieutenant Jerry Rawlings, was followed by the summary trial and execution of three former heads of state (all generals) and other senior officials of the former regimes in an effort to 'cleanse' the nation of corruption. There was, however, no delay in the restoration of civilian rule; elections were duly held and a new government with Dr Hilla Limann as President assumed office on 24 September 1979. The new constitution provided for a multiparty system but in other features suggested 'Washington' rather than 'Westminster'. Thus the office of Prime Minister disappeared and was replaced by an executive President, directly elected every four years; President and ministers were not to sit in Parliament.[4]

Unlike Ghana, Nigeria had experienced almost fourteen years of uninterrupted military government when civilian constitutional government was restored on 1 October 1979. Although not without blemish, the Nigerian military government had some important achievements to its credit, aided, admittedly, by the financial strength provided by the country's newly developed oil resources. The civil war involving the attempt of Biafra to secede from the Federation had ended in 1970, and a successful policy of reconciliation minimised the legacy of the bitter conflict. The old ill-balanced regional structure, in which the Federation had been effectively dominated by the vast Northern Region, was replaced by a nineteen-state system. Important reforms in such fields as local government and land tenure were carried out. The military government also presided over the elaborate and lengthy consultative process by which a new constitution was drafted.

The shift to 'Washington' which has been observed in the case of Ghana was more pronounced in the case of Nigeria. Indeed, the 1979 constitution marks a decisive move away from the 'Westminster' style of parliamentary democracy with which so many Commonwealth countries began their independent life. The President is chief executive and Commander-in-Chief of the armed forces, elected for a fixed four-year, and once-renewable, term; each state has a directly elected State Governor; the Federal legislature is composed of a Senate (with equal representation from each state) and a House of Representatives with single-member constituencies; ministers are appointed by the President but subject to confirmation by the Senate; they are excluded from the legislature.

The new constitution, however, does contain a number of features which reflect the special problems of Nigeria and which show an attempt to learn the lessons of history. Thus, following precedents from the one-party systems of Tanzania and Zambia, the constitution prescribes a code of conduct designed to impose basic standards of personal integrity upon all 'public officers'. There is also an ingenious attempt to ensure that political activity is carried on through the medium of political parties which are truly national rather than, as in the case of the First Republic, largely reflecting the sectional interests of a particular region or ethnic grouping.[5]

For the student of Commonwealth history, therefore, the African experience in the 1970s shows state structures evolving away from that Westminster model which was more or less imposed at independence at the beginning of the previous decade. The citizen's right to 'participate by means of free and democratic political processes' referred to in the 1971 Commonwealth Declaration found expression in the one-party participatory democracies of east and central Africa, and in the 'Washington-model' constitutions developed in Nigeria and Ghana. Although the forms might change, there were good grounds for believing, at the end of the decade, that democracy in Commonwealth Africa would not prove the sickly and frail implantation that many had predicted as a succession of countries had earlier succumbed to military rule.

If the second post-independence decade ended on an optimistic note in Commonwealth Africa, reinforced by Zimbabwe's achievement of independence (see below), the experience of the South Asian Commonwealth does not suggest that the third decade of freedom is likely to be easy. The decade opened with signs of a crisis in Pakistan leading, in 1971, to armed conflict between the West and East wings of the country and renewed hostilities between Pakistan and India, as the latter went to the assistance of the Bengalis of East Pakistan.

In December 1971, the former East Pakistan emerged as the independent state of Bangladesh. Pakistan, whose territory now comprised only the former province of West Pakistan, withdrew from the Commonwealth and, after the usual processes of consultation, Bangladesh was admitted in her own right in April 1972. The new member's problems were desperate. One of the largest Commonwealth states in terms of population, Bangladesh is uncomfortably the poorest in terms of Gross National Product per capita, with less than half that of Tanzania.[6] It was hardly surprising that the politics of the early post-independence years were violent and stormy. The nationalist leader and first Prime Minister, Sheikh Mujib, assumed sweeping presidential powers in 1975 only to be assassinated in a military coup later in the year. Coup and counter-coup then followed in a period of violence and confusion until in 1976 a military government headed by General Ziaur became firmly established. Ziaur's assumption of the presidency was made respectable by success in a contested popular election in 1978 and in a parliamentary election in 1979. Democratic forms were thus rather shakily re-established.

Bangladesh's giant neighbour, India, the largest parliamentary democracy in the world, found the third decade of independence a crisis-ridden experience. In 1969, the monolithic Congress Party, which had governed India without a break since independence, split into two wings. Although the ruling wing under the Prime

Minister, Mrs Indira Gandhi, won an overwhelming victory in the 1971 General Election, she ran into increasing difficulties in the fields of law and order and economic policy. Mrs Gandhi's response was authoritarian – in 1975 a State of Emergency was proclaimed, and in the following year, the life of Parliament was extended and the constitution was amended to strengthen the power of the central government. When, however, it appeared that the democratic forms were endangered by an increasingly authoritarian regime relying on detentions, censorship and the arbitrary imposition of policies such as male sterilisation, in 1977 Mrs Gandhi put her case to the people in a general election which resulted in a first ever defeat for Congress (Mrs Gandhi lost her own seat) and a decisive victory for the newly formed opposition grouping, the Janata Front.

Indian democracy may be said to have come of age in that peaceful transfer of power, which reflected credit on the defeated Mrs Gandhi, who had wielded near-absolute authority. Also significant was the carefully maintained neutrality of India's military forces: that apparently complete detachment from the political crisis provided a unique and welcome change in third-world power struggles. Mrs Gandhi's restraint was later to pay handsome dividends in one of the most remarkable political come-backs of Commonwealth history. The Janata government broke up in factional confusion within two years of its triumph, and Mrs Gandhi was returned triumphantly to power by an overwhelming popular vote. India remains the largest working democracy in the world, but Mrs Gandhi was able to strengthen the powers of the central government on the basis that only firm leadership can tackle the enormous economic and social problems that India faces.

In Sri Lanka (known as Ceylon until 1972) the decade saw a rapid series of political and constitutional upheavals. Until 1972, Ceylon retained the constitution in force at independence in 1948, with a Governor-General representing the Queen and a typical 'Westminster'-style prime ministerial system. Indeed Ceylon was cited as the classic 'new Commonwealth' example of a functioning multiparty parliamentary system: four general elections between 1956 and 1970 had on each occasion resulted in the defeat of the governing party and in a peaceful transfer of power to the opposition.

The victors of the 1970 election, Mrs S. Bandaranaike and her Sri Lanka Freedom Party, were committed to drastic constitutional reforms. These were effected in a manner which deliberately broke the chain of legal continuity with the colonial past, being adopted by a Constituent Assembly which had no formal link with the old Parliament. In 1972 Sri Lanka became a republic within the Commonwealth. After Mrs Bandaranaike in turn suffered a crushing defeat in the 1977 election at the hands of Mr J. R. Jayewardene's United National Party, further constitutional changes introduced a 'Gaullist' executive presidency. Mr Jayewardene assumed office as executive President in 1978.

Commonwealth members of the 'class of 1960' in East Asia and the West Indies on the whole avoided radical political and constitutional change, although stability was not always easily maintained. Thus communal disturbances in Malaysia in 1969 meant that the country began the decade under emergency rule. However, the authority of Parliament and the Cabinet was restored in 1971, and increasing prosperity appeared to ameliorate communal tensions between Chinese and *Bumiputras* (Malays). In some countries, particularly in the West Indies, economic difficulties enflamed discontent among the poor and the unemployed and contributed to increasing lawlessness. Thus Jamaica, while retaining the parliamentary system established at independence in 1962, was obliged to take apparently draconian measures against gangsters, including the setting up of a special 'Gun Court' in 1974. In the autumn of 1980 a violent general election campaign resulted in a landslide victory for the right-wing Labour Party. In general the West Indies remained a bastion of the 'Westminster' system of government, although Trinidad and Tobago in 1976 made the small change from monarchy to non-executive presidency as a republic within the Commonwealth, and Guyana, a republic since 1970, in 1980 adopted a new constitution providing for the establishment of an executive presidency.

Throughout the 1970s Cyprus continued to provide one of the most intractable problems to face the Commonwealth. The already difficult situation created by the breakdown in 1963 of the independence constitutional settlement between the Greek and Turkish communities was exacerbated by the dramatic events of 1974, involving a temporarily successful Greek coup against President Makarios, and a Turkish invasion of northern Cyprus. The island was then effectively partitioned between the area controlled by the (Greek Cypriot) government of Cyprus recognised by other Commonwealth states, and that under the control of an administration claiming to be that of the 'Turkish Federated

State' of Cyprus. Although the Cyprus problem was regarded primarily as a United Nations matter involving non-Commonwealth parties, the issue was discussed regularly at Heads of Government meetings, and at the Kingston Meeting in 1975 a Commonwealth Committee on Cyprus was established to assist UN efforts to achieve a settlement.

So far in this chapter the emphasis has been on the problems of nation-building in those Commonwealth countries which achieved independence in the period after 1945. In the older Commonwealth countries, however, the period was remarkable for the extent to which long-established constitutional structures were called into question. Issues which a decade earlier were to be found discussed only in scholarly works aimed primarily at students of constitutional law were now debated in the columns of daily newspapers and on television screens.

In Britain, which had long been open to the accusation of declining to take the constitutional medicine which she happily prescribed for others, a major debate was initiated as to the need for a written constitution incorporating an entrenched bill of rights. A Royal Commission on the Constitution reported in 1973 after lengthy deliberations. Elaborate statutory provision was made for the introduction of 'devolved' government in Wales and Scotland. These proposals, although placed on the statute book in 1978, failed to receive the necessary endorsement in referendums held in 1979. If these proposals had been implemented, however, the United Kingdom might have moved towards a quasi-federal structure. Finally, the perennial issue of the reform or abolition of the House of Lords erupted at the Labour Party Conference of 1980.[7]

Fundamental constitutional issues were also matters of controversy in Canada and Australia. Canada was faced with a threat to her very existence as a federal nation by a strong separatist movement in French-speaking Quebec. In a 1980 referendum the people of Quebec narrowly rejected the provincial government's request for a mandate to negotiate a new status of 'sovereignty-association' which would have provided for political independence, though cushioned by continuing close economic links with the rest of Canada.

The Quebec issue served to focus attention on what appeared to many Canadians to be a major constitutional anomaly. Under section 7 of the Statute of Westminster,[8] the United Kingdom Parliament retained exclusive power to amend the British North

America Acts which contained the constitution of Canada. Although by the British North America Act 1949, the Parliament of Canada acquired exclusive authority to amend much of the constitution, certain important matters relating, among other things, to provincial powers and rights, remained reserved to the Westminster Parliament. There was, of course, nothing unusual about the necessity to refer to British legislation when considering the constitution of an independent Commonwealth country, since many of them retain constitutions which were first promulgated as schedules to British Orders in Council. What was unique about the Canadian situation was the local parliament's lack of complete competence in the field of constitutional amendment. This position, which had been deliberately preserved as a way of 'entrenching' the constitutional standing of the provinces in 1949, was seen as an affront to Canadian sovereignty and national pride in the 1970s. The decade ended, therefore, with the launching, by Pierre Trudeau's Liberal government, of a comprehensive plan for constitutional reform. This would include the redefinition of the position of the Crown and the Governor-General in an effort to placate those who resented the connection with the 'British' monarch.

Despite the personal success of the Queen's tour of Australia as part of the Silver Jubilee celebrations of 1977, there was some indication of a growth of republican sentiment in Australia. Vague doubts as to the relevance of the monarchy to modern Australian society were given a political edge by the dismissal of a Prime Minister by the Governor-General in 1975.

A political crisis had been created by the refusal of the opposition-controlled Senate to pass the government's budget bills. When the Labour Prime Minister, Gough Whitlam declined to resolve the issue by asking for a dissolution of Parliament, he was dismissed by Sir John Kerr, and replaced by the Opposition leader, Malcolm Fraser. The latter subsequently won an overwhelming victory at the polls.

In a sense, therefore, Kerr's action was endorsed by the electorate, and he thus avoided the humiliation suffered by Lord Byng in Canada in 1926.[9] However, the 1975 crisis aroused bitter controversy, particularly as Kerr had been appointed on Whitlam's recommendation. Since the position of the monarch's representative was involved, the crisis inevitably brought in question the position of the monarch. The matter was, of course, purely an internal Australian affair involving the Governor-General's powers under the Australian constitution. A similar situation could have arisen if Australia had had a non-executive president as head of state. Many Australians, however, were startled by the dismissal of an elected Prime Minister in a manner which was unthinkable in the United Kingdom, and some came to feel that only if Australia became a republic could it be truly independent.

The strengthening of republican sentiment in two of the 'old Dominions' requires some reflections upon the position of the monarchy in the Commonwealth in 1980. Once, acceptance of a common allegiance to the Crown had been a *sine qua non* of membership. As we have seen, the exception made to permit India to remain a member of the Commonwealth when she became a republic in 1950 became a routine procedure in the 1960s. Of the fifteen countries of which the Queen was Head of State at the end of 1980, four comprised the 'old Commonwealth' (the United Kingdom, Canada, Australia and New Zealand) and eight were in their first decade of independence.

It was possible in 1980 to envisage a situation when the monarch's dominions might be confined to the United Kingdom, her remaining dependencies and, perhaps, New Zealand. For the moment, however, there was continued acceptance by all members of the Commonwealth, whatever their own political status, of the Queen's titular position as Head of Commonwealth. This position implied no threat to the sovereign independence of members and would be acceptable to Australian republicans and Quebec separatists alike.

It would have been unfortunate if 'Commonwealth' sentiment in Australia and Canada had been affected by resentment against the retention of the 'British' monarchy. Although a strenuous programme of royal tours in the 1970s apparently revitalised the roles of 'Queen of Australia' and 'Queen of Canada', the celebration of the Jubilee in June 1977, reflected the overwhelmingly British character of the occasion. In contrast to the Jubilees of 1897 and 1935, and even to the Queen's own Coronation in 1953, the ceremonial processions on Jubilee Day included only one contingent of Canadian 'Mounties' as a reminder of the once-extensive dominions beyond the seas.

Although not matching the dramatic increase in Commonwealth membership in the decade ending in 1970 (when the pace of decolonisation was most rapid, and numbers increased from eleven to thirty-two), the decade ending in 1980 saw numbers rise from thirty-two to forty-four. If the health of the club is measured by ability to attract new members, therefore, the Commonwealth is clearly in good shape. All the countries which attained independence from Britain elected to apply, as did the former Anglo-French condominium of the New Hebrides (Vanuatu), and Australia's former dependency of Papua New Guinea. As noted earlier, Bangladesh, having broken away from the rest of Pakistan, also obtained admission. In 1980, there existed the strong possibility that Namibia might wish to join the Commonwealth on independence.

The decolonisation process in the 1970s did not involve – except in the special case of Zimbabwe to which we shall return – the 'struggle' for independence. As George (subsequently Lord) Thomson, the last British Commonwealth Secretary, put it: 'We shall not stand in the way of any territory which wishes to proceed to independence'. Thus the test was the wishes of the inhabitants. The metropolitan power would no longer decline to grant independence on the grounds, for example, that the proposed new state would not be viable economically, or was too small. The path of constitutional advance was therefore generally smooth and swift, with the active encouragement of a colonial power anxious to dispose of the last vestiges of the imperial burden.

Apart from Papua New Guinea (population two and a half million) and Zimbabwe (population approximately seven million), all the ex-dependencies achieving independence were small island communities with populations ranging from 200,000 (Bahamas and Solomons) to barely 10,000 (Tuvalu). All were fitted out with variants of the Westminster-model constitution, although, in the case of very small territories, some attempt was made to scale-down the institutions in a manner appropriate for local conditions: thus the Parliament of Tuvalu consists of twelve members, including a Prime Minister, four other ministers and Mr Speaker. A major problem in dealing with these small island communities was their intense individualism. Government by the representatives of a distant and 'neutral' colonial power might be acceptable; government by people from a neighbouring island certainly was not. The intractable nature of problems of this kind was demonstrated in 1969, when Anguilla, part of the Associated State of St Christopher, Nevis and Anguilla, revolted and had to be placed again under direct British rule.[10] The former colony of the Gilbert and Ellice Islands provides another example. At the request of the Ellice Islanders, and with the consent of the Gilbertese, the colony, with a total population of less than 65,000, was partitioned: the

Ellice Islands (Tuvalu) and the Gilberts (Kiribati) proceeded separately to independence in 1978 and 1979. A further obstacle to the independence of the Gilberts had been the desire of the Banaban people of Ocean Island (Banaba) to be excluded from the new state. The Banabans had attracted considerable support and sympathy in the United Kingdom as a result of a mammoth High Court action against the British Government over phosphate-mining on the island. Eventually, however, the British Government, professing to be guided by the wishes of the people as a whole within the existing boundaries, decided that Banaba should be included within the new state of Kiribati.

In 1980, an even more complex situation arose as progress to independence of the Anglo-French condominium of the New Hebrides was for a time threatened by a secessionist revolt on one of the islands of the group. The authority of the local government was only re-established after the dispatch of British, French and, subsequently, Papua New Guinea troops. Again, as the Commonwealth Secretary-General, Shridath Ramphal, so eloquently put it, a crisis had been produced by that 'false and dangerous melody, the siren song of secession sung to the tune of self-determination'.[11]

This proliferation of potentially unstable 'mini-states' in the Commonwealth reflected the failure to develop any viable alternative to full sovereign independence for communities which would have been regarded in the previous decade as incapable of sustaining that status. Thus, in the West Indies, the failure of the federal experiment of 1958–62 was followed by the unsatisfactory status of 'association' under the West Indies Act of 1967.[12] The Anguilla affair exposed the possible embarrassment for Britain of the retention of residual responsibility for security in such circumstances, while continued colonial status, however well disguised, could not satisfy local aspirations. One by one, therefore, the associated states moved to full independence: Grenada in 1974, Dominica in 1978, and St Lucia and St Vincent in 1979.

Antigua took the same path in 1981, while St Christopher's progress remained blocked by the problem of Anguilla and also by strong separatist feelings on the third island, Nevis. The transition to independence had been accompanied by riots and other signs of political unrest on a number of the islands. After independence, island politics remained as stormy as the climate: in 1979, the premier of Grenada, Sir Eric Gairy, was ousted by the 'People's

Revolutionary Army' and Mr Patrick John, premier of Dominica, was forced to resign after troops had fired on anti-government demonstrators with fatal results.

For the last and most dramatic story of decolonisation of the decade, however, we must return to Africa, and to Zimbabwe – ruled since 1965 by the rebellious white minority regime claiming after 1969 to be the 'Republic of Rhodesia'. It hardly seemed likely, in any circumstances which could be envisaged at that time, that the regime would ever be compelled to haul down its flag, return to the colonial fold and accept an independence constitution from Britain in the traditional way. Sanctions had proved ineffective (partly, it was to be revealed later, because Britain herself had failed to discourage British-owned companies from supplying oil to Rhodesia),[13] the economy was prosperous and the regime appeared to be in unchallenged control.

The settlement reached with the regime in 1971 by Sir Alec Douglas-Home, Foreign and Commonwealth Secretary in Edward Heath's Conservative government, appeared to African Commonwealth members to be a sell-out to the rebels. The African states had made clear to Heath at the Singapore Heads of Government meeting their continued insistence on NIBMAR – No Independence Before Majority African Rule – whereas Douglas-Home accepted a settlement based on the 1970 rebel constitution which was unlikely to produce majority rule until at least thirty years after independence. Britain had acknowledged at the Singapore Conference, however, that any settlement would have to be acceptable to the people of Rhodesia as a whole.

A Commission under a British Judge, Lord Pearce, accordingly visited Rhodesia and found that African opinion, mobilised under Abel Muzorewa, a Methodist bishop, was overwhelmingly against the proposals. This rejection marked the abandonment of British attempts to produce a constitutional settlement through bilateral dealings with the Smith regime.

From 1973 onwards, the Smith regime was faced with an intensification of the armed struggle by African nationalist guerrillas. The latter's effectiveness was greatly increased – and the security of the white regime undermined – by the collapse of Portuguese colonial rule in Mozambique in 1975 and the establishment there of an African Marxist government. The British government (a minority Labour administration under Harold Wilson had returned to office after the February 1974 general election) now accepted that any independence settlement would have to provide for immediate majority rule. The principle of majority rule was also conceded by the Smith regime, faced with an escalating guerrilla war and international pressure not only from Britain but also from the United States and South Africa, whose governments were both anxious to 'liquidate' an increasingly embarrassing problem.

The various parties to the dispute, however, remained far apart on the manner of the implementation of majority rule, as was shown by two months of fruitless wrangling at a conference at Geneva in the autumn of 1976. This first attempt to negotiate a settlement involving all the parties – including the African nationalist leaders and the regime – was followed by a period in which the prospects of such a settlement appeared to recede as the various parties pursued divergent objectives. The two principal African nationalist groups – Joshua Nkomo's ZAPU and Robert Mugabe's ZANU – had formed a precarious alliance as the Patriotic Front (PF), and remained committed to a military victory. They accordingly intensified their war effort.

In September 1977 the British Government published a set of detailed constitutional proposals as part of an Anglo-American initiative. The proposals involved the temporary establishment of direct British colonial rule prior to independence, and were rejected by both the Smith regime and the Patriotic Front.

The illegal regime's more positive response was an agreement, signed in March 1978, with a number of African political leaders inside the country – including Bishop Abel Muzorewa, who had played such a prominent part in the defeat of the Douglas-Home proposals. This 'internal settlement' provided for the drafting of a constitution claiming to give effect to the principle of majority rule, for the holding of elections based on universal adult suffrage, and for the transition to 'independence'.

Although the Patriotic Front boycotted the proceedings and continued the war, Bishop Muzorewa assumed office as 'Prime Minister of Zimbabwe Rhodesia' on 1 June 1979. Ian Smith, who had once ruled out African government in his lifetime, nevertheless felt able to accept ministerial office in the Muzorewa government. Smith's presence was an indication of the extent to which effective power had remained in European hands. There were twenty-eight white reserved seats in the 100-member legislature, and the constitution (which for ten years could not be changed without the approval of the European members) firmly entrenched white domination of the civil service, the judiciary and the armed forces.[14]

As Commonwealth Heads of Government assembled for their meeting at Lusaka in August 1979, therefore, a negotiated settlement of the Rhodesia problem acceptable to all parties – a settlement which alone could end the war – seemed as far away as ever. To some pessimists, it appeared that the Rhodesian crisis was finally to bring about the break-up of the Commonwealth which had lived under its shadow since 1965. Certainly a British move to legitimise the Muzorewa regime – a move which had been on the cards since the return of a Conservative government to power in May 1979 – would have created a bitter rift between Britain and the 'front-line' Commonwealth African states and other members, such as Nigeria, who strongly supported the Patriotic Front.

Despite these gloomy forebodings, the Lusaka Conference achieved a spectacular success. It produced a formula which proved acceptable to all parties and which led to a constitutional conference, a cease-fire, free elections and the emergence of an independent Zimbabwe within eight months of the Lusaka meeting. The way that the formula emerged demonstrated the unique character and value of the Commonwealth consultative process. Discussions took place not in large plenary meetings at which each contributor felt obliged to restate known positions, but in small informal groups. During the week-end 'retreat' at State House for heads of delegation and their spouses, much of the groundwork was done for the final Lusaka accord on Zimbabwe.

It is in this context that the ability of the Commonwealth to call on the experience of leaders of countries from all over the globe, and at every stage of economic development, is particularly valuable. Thus leading roles in hammering out the agreed formula for the settlement of the future of an African country, Zimbabwe, were played by the Prime Ministers of Australia, Malcolm Fraser, and of Jamaica, Michael Manley.

The implementation of the Lusaka agreement was not an easy task. The Constitutional Conference, for which all parties to the conflict assembled in September 1979 at the traditional venue, Lancaster House, took over three months to reach agreement.[15] The terms of the independence constitution, the interim arrangements for the period during which fresh elections would be held, and the cease-fire provisions each in turn threatened to prove fatal stumbling blocks to a settlement.

The Patriotic Front leaders, Robert Mugabe and Joshua Nkomo, were deeply suspicious of the British proposals, particularly those relating to the cease-fire. These involved the concentration of the Patriotic Front forces in assembly points, where they might be at the mercy of the Rhodesian airforce if the cease-fire collapsed. The Patriotic Front only accepted these arrangements after the British government had taken the calculated gamble of sending out as governor, Lord Soames (himself a senior Cabinet minister), to Salisbury on 12 December in order to bring the rebellion to an end and accomplish the restoration of constitutional government in the 'colony of Southern Rhodesia'.

As the last British proconsul in Africa, Lord Soames's task was as formidable as that which had faced any of his predecessors – Cromer, Milner, Lugard, Cohen and the rest. In theory, his powers were absolute. In practice, he and his small team of civil and military advisers relied on the co-operation of the administration, police and security services of the former 'rebel' regime. The immediate aftermath of a bitter and bloody civil war was hardly a propitious time for the holding of the 'free and fair elections' specified at Lusaka.

The election campaign was marred by a good deal of violence and alleged intimidation by supporters of the former 'Prime Minister' Bishop Muzorewa and by those of the two wings of the Patriotic Front (Mr Mugabe and Mr Nkomo fought the election separately). Remarkably, however, the great majority of the Patriotic Front guerrilla forces assembled at the designated camps and remained there during the campaign: the cease-fire held. The election in February 1980, produced a clear majority for Mr Mugabe's ZANU (PF) party and he was invited by Lord Soames to assume office as Prime Minister. In April, Zimbabwe at last attained legal independence as the forty-third member state of the Commonwealth.

There were many factors in the successful accomplishment of what had seemed to many an impossible task, not least the restraint and statesmanship shown by the Patriotic Front leaders in accepting a peaceful – and for them risky – solution to a conflict which they appeared bound to win by military means. For Britain, the Foreign Secretary, Lord Carrington, by his conduct of the Lancaster House negotiations, and Lord Soames, by his performance as governor in the crucial interim period, showed great political courage, diplomatic skill and toughness when most needed. In the final settlement of the Rhodesian independence issue, therefore, British statesmen did something to redeem the sad record of their predecessors whose repeated failures in this regard had so discredited Britain in the eyes of the Commonwealth and the world.

The Commonwealth as an institution also gained enormously in prestige from the key role it played from Lusaka onwards. The Secretary-General, Mr Shridath Ramphal, and leaders of several Commonwealth governments were indefatigable behind the scenes at Lancaster House in averting the breakdown so often threatened during the course of the conference. During the period leading up to the election, a crucial role was played in Rhodesia by the Commonwealth Observer Group.

The Group was set up in the terms of the Lusaka Accord and the Lancaster House Agreement, to monitor the conduct of the election, which it was a British responsibility to supervise. The observers were drawn from eleven different Commonwealth countries. Their investigations often served to diffuse crises provoked by allegations of intimidation and unfair electoral practices. Their interim report, issued on the eve of polling, played a key role in securing the acceptance of the result by all participants and by the international community. This report confirmed that in all the circumstances the election could be considered 'free and fair'.[16] A valuable role was also played by the soldiers from four Commonwealth countries (in addition to Britain) who participated in the monitoring force set up to oversee the cease-fire during the election period.

Thus Britain performed her final major act of decolonisation with the active assistance and participation of her Commonwealth partners. In a sense, too, Britain was accountable to them for the implementation of the Lusaka Accord. Although not legally binding, that Accord provided the framework within which the Lancaster House Agreement was negotiated and carried out. There was some irony in the fact that the Commonwealth, the very existence of which had been endangered for many years by the Rhodesian issue, should eventually draw fresh strength from the resolution of the conflict.

The virtues of the Commonwealth 'method', with its emphasis on informal consultation and, in the case of the Commonwealth Observer Group, *ad hoc* improvision from small resources, were shown to compare favourably with the cumbersome and over rigid procedures of the United Nations. The subsequent invitation to send a Commonwealth observer group to monitor the Uganda election of December 1980 (the first since independence in 1962) suggested that the success of the Rhodesian exercise may have set a useful precedent. Even after independence, Commonwealth countries may need help of this kind to strengthen the delicate process whereby their people are offered a genuinely free political choice.

The long-delayed achievement of independence in Zimbabwe did not, of course, mean the end of Britain's colonial responsibilities. At the end of 1980, the list of Britain's dependent territories, excluding the Associated States of Antigua and St Christopher, Nevis, Anguilla, the State of Brunei, for whose external affairs Britain will remain responsible until 1983, and the sovereign base areas in Cyprus, comprised the following:

|  | *Population in thousands*<br>*1977* |
|---|---|
| Belize | 149 |
| Bermuda | 58 |
| British Virgin Islands | 12 |
| Cayman Islands | 11 |
| Falkland Islands | 2 |
| Gibraltar | 30 |
| (Hong Kong | 4514) |
| Montserrat | 13 |
| Pitcairn | 0.064 |
| St Helena | 5 |
| Turks and Caicos Islands | 6 |
| Total (excluding Hong Kong) | 286,000 |

(Taken from *A Year Book of the Commonwealth*, HMSO, 1979)

A number of these territories are effectively excluded from progress to independence by external factors. Hong Kong, immensely wealthy and by far the largest remaining dependency, has its constitutional development frozen at a pre-representative stage by the sensitivity of its huge neighbour, China. Hong Kong, it appears, will remain a British colony for as long as China wishes. It is impossible to speculate what the Chinese attitude will be when the 'lease' of 'The New Territories expires in 1997.[17] Certainly, however, relations between Britain and China improved enormously during the 1970s, after the low point during the Cultural Revolution which inspired the destruction of the British mission in Pekin and serious riots in Hong Kong. The governor of Hong Kong was, by the end of the decade, a welcome visitor to the Chinese capital. The new Chinese leadership after the death of Chairman Mao appeared to place particular value on Hong Kong's role as a window on to the capitalist world.

Independence also appeared ruled out for the Falkland Islands, over which Argentina continued to press her claim to sovereignty, and for Gibraltar, where Spain was the claimant. In both cases, Britain was committed to respecting the wishes of the inhabitants who were generally opposed to any change in status. Belize (formerly British Honduras) was also kept in the incongruous status of a colony enjoying internal self-government by the claims to the territory of neighbouring Guatemala. The latter's pretensions necessitated a British military presence in the colony, a commitment which increased the British desire for disengagement. Although in 1978 an old-fashioned attempt to buy off Guatemalan opposition to independence with a slice of territory foundered on understandable Belizean opposition. Even though Guatemala remained unreconciled, Belize, with strong Commonwealth and international support, eventually took its place as an independent member of the Commonwealth in 1981.

In the case of Bermuda, which also enjoyed a large measure of self-government, the problem was internal rather than external. Racial and other social and economic tensions produced serious disturbances in 1968 and 1977, and the predominantly white governing élite preferred the security of colonial status. However, it seemed by 1980 that full independence was unlikely to be long delayed. The remaining small West Indian island dependencies were likely to follow the same path, despite doubts about the security and economic viability of microstates in such a volatile region. The Turks and Caicos Islands well illustrate the problem. In 1980, the British government incurred strong criticism from the 'aid lobby' for fostering a scheme whereby a major tourist resort would be developed there by the 'Club Méditerrané'. Presumably the attraction of the scheme from the British point of view was that it provided the islands, otherwise without economic resources, with the prospect of infrastructural development and income with which to sustain progress to independence.

Certainly, as we have seen, successive British governments in the 1970s made little secret of their desire to liquidate the remaining colonial responsibilities. However, the commitment not to force any territory into independence or into association with another state against the wishes of the inhabitants meant that the 'imperial' power was no longer even able to dictate the pace of her withdrawal from empire. It appears that even at the end of the 1980s, the Union Jack will still fly over Hong Kong, Pitcairn, St Helena and, perhaps, the Falklands and Gibraltar.

The process of decolonisation described above had a continuing impact on the nature of the Commonwealth association. The influx of small and economically weak states created a demand for increased emphasis on the functional, co-operative aspects of Commonwealth activity. Suspicion that the latter necessarily had some kind of 'neo-colonial' connotation also diminished on the part of established members of the 'Afro-Asian' Commonwealth. The numerical dominance of developing, non-aligned countries was now overwhelming. The Commonwealth consensus now reflected their concerns and their priorities. It was the latter, too, which determined functional and institutional developments, as traditional links, often involving a pivotal British role, disappeared.

Thus, in the economic sphere, the decade saw a major landmark in the accession of the United Kingdom to the European Economic Community in 1973. This signalled the end of the system of Commonwealth preferences and associated agreements, such as the Commonwealth Sugar Agreement. Also of great significance was the end of the role of sterling as a reserve currency for most of the Commonwealth. Bilateral links with Britain ceased to dominate the trade patterns of old Commonwealth countries such as Australia and New Zealand. Although Britain was still Australia's largest single customer in 1964, by 1977 exports to Britain were less than half those to the United States and one-eighth of those to Japan.[18]

Any lingering idea of the Commonwealth as a tariff and monetary union was now firmly buried. Trade co-operation between Britain and the developing countries of the Afro/Caribbean/Pacific Commonwealth was now to be regulated within the framework of the Lomé Convention signed in February 1975, between the European Community and forty-six 'ACP' countries. These latter included the former French and Belgian colonies in Africa, while the agreement excluded the Asian Commonwealth. Lomé thus cut across traditional Commonwealth links. A fresh

The Commonwealth Revived, 1971-80                    139

treaty (Lomé II) was signed in 1980, after much bitter wrangling. The 1979 Commonwealth Conference recorded the 'strong dissatisfaction of Commonwealth ACP countries with the outcome of the negotiations'.[19]

These fundamental changes did not mean that questions of economic co-operation and development ceased to be a Commonwealth concern. Indeed, the decade saw the emergence of the Commonwealth as a key forum for consultation and research regarding matters arising out of the 'North/South' dialogue – the global problem of economic relations between the few rich nations and the many poor ones. The particular value of the Commonwealth association was again demonstrated: a voluntary association not bound together in a political or trading bloc, and containing representative examples of states from every point of the North/South spectrum.

A perusal of the final communiqués of the five Heads of Government meetings of the decade – Singapore, 1971, Ottawa, 1973, Kingston, 1975, Londond, 1977 and Lusaka, 1979 – shows the increasing importance of questions of economic development and related questions in the deliberations of Commonwealth leaders. At the Kingston meeting, Heads of Government set up a committee of experts to draw up a programme of practical measures directed at closing the gap between rich and poor countries in the context of the establishment of a new international economic order. This committee's findings were a precursor to those of the Brandt Commission, on which the Commonwealth Secretary-General, Shridath Ramphal, was one of six representatives from Commonwealth countries.[20] At Lusaka, in 1979, a further experts' report was commissioned to assist Commonwealth governments in their preparation for the Special 'Development' Session of the UN General Assembly in 1980.

Thus the Commonwealth forum was a valuable opportunity for consultations outside the framework of such institutionalised negotiations as the United Nations Conference on Trade and Development (UNCTAD), or the Conference on International Economic Co-operation (CIEC). This Commonwealth consultative process was not confined to the Heads of Government meetings. For example, Commonwealth finance ministers met annually to exchange and co-ordinate views on international monetary and financial issues on the eve of the annual meetings of the World Bank and the International Monetary Fund (IMF). As Ramphal said in

1978, 'The Commonwealth cannot negotiate for the world; but it can help the world to negotiate'.

The role of the Commonwealth was not confined to consultation. One of the most remarkable indications of the revival of the Commonwealth during the decade was afforded in the field of functional co-operation. The Commonwealth Fund for Technical Co-operation (CFTC) was set up in 1971 to assist the developing countries of the Commonwealth in the provision of technical assistance. The CFTC is not simply another medium for the doling out of aid from rich to poor countries. Members at every stage of development help to provide money, staff and facilities. The Fund is administered by the Commonwealth Secretariat in a way which has managed to avoid the usual harsh divide between donor and recipient countries. The emphasis has been rather on mutual co-operation and assistance. By 1980, specialists deployed by the Fund to meet specific manpower needs had been drawn from twenty-nine countries, and over 58 per cent of the experts themselves came from developing countries.[21]

The most unusual, perhaps even controversial, aspect of the CFTC's activities has centred on the Technical Assistance Group (TAG), a consultative group of economists, lawyers and tax specialists on whom Commonwealth governments can call for help in sensitive matters involving the exploration of their natural resources – for example, the drafting of mineral legislation or negotiations with transnational corporations. Many small states cannot hope to match the latter's resources in expertise and TAG has been widely used by African, Caribbean and Pacific Commonwealth governments.

As reflected in institutions such as the CFTC, the Secretariat became during the 1970s much more than an administrative office for processing inter-Commonwealth communications and servicing meetings. The evolution of the role of the Secretariat in part reflected the dynamic impact of the second Secretary-General, Shridath Ramphal. He succeeded the distinguished Canadian diplomat, Arnold Smith, in 1975, and was elected to a second five-year term at the Lusaka Heads of Government Meeting in 1979. Ramphal brought to the office his prestige and authority as a respected international statesman; he had been Foreign Minister of Guyana, and was twice elected Vice-President of the UN General Assembly. He played a major role in the negotiations which led to the signing of the first Lomé Convention. With his background as a

leading advocate of third world causes, and as a citizen of a small
developing country, he was able to assume a more active involvement in issues of common Commonwealth concern without arous-
ing the suspicions of member states – suspicions which had delayed
the creation of the office of Secretary-General until 1965. He was
thus free to advocate the cause of the developing countries in the
search for a 'new international economic order' and to play a
prominent part as a member of the Brandt Commission. Most
significantly, perhaps, he was able to play a key mediating role
during the tortuous and crisis-ridden negotiations which led to the
Lancaster House Agreement on Zimbabwe in December 1979.

Examining the range of Commonwealth activities reviewed in
Ramphal's long report presented to Heads of Government at
Lusaka, it does not appear fanciful or overoptimistic to see clear
evidence that the Commonwealth, once regarded by many as a
rather embarrassing relic of Empire which would quickly, and
possibly quietly, fade away, has entered the 1980s with healthy new
tissue growing on its old bones.[22] It is clear that, in many
practical ways, the Commonwealth has acquired the capacity to be
supportive of its newest and weakest members.

The Commonwealth has also developed a special sensitivity with
regard to issues which are of particular concern to third world
members, but of common concern to all. This applies not only in the
economic sphere, as described above, but also in the strength of the
Commonwealth commitment to oppose racism. Thus the London
Heads of Government Meeting in 1977 produced a statement on
*apartheid* in sport, whereby member governments accepted a
commitment to withhold any form of support for racist sport, and to
discourage contact or competition by their nationals with sporting
organisations or sportsmen from South Africa or from any other
country where sports were organised on the basis of race, colour or
ethnic origin.[23] The 1979 Lusaka meeting in turn agreed a
Declaration of the Commonwealth on Racism and Racial
Prejudice, the broad terms of which amounted to a Commonwealth
version of the Universal Declaration of Human Rights.
Subsequently, the Secretary-General was authorised to set up a
working party to consider the desirability of establishing some
formal Commonwealth body to monitor the observance of human
rights in the Commonwealth.

The idea of a 'Commonwealth Human Rights Court' may yet
encounter too much opposition, but it is a significant indication of

the positive role seen for the Commonwealth in the 1980s that such a proposal should reach the discussion stage at official level. Certainly, the Commonwealth is not past the age of child-bearing in terms of institutional development, as witness the innovation in 1978 of the Heads of Government Regional Meeting. Heads of Government of twelve countries from Asia and the Pacific – together with the Secretary-General – met in Sydney, Australia, for four days of discussion which focused on the particular problems of developing countries within the region and on ways of improving regional economic and functional co-operation. Other practical issues, such as the improvement of co-operation in combating terrorism and illicit drug-trafficking, were referred to working parties. A further meeting took place in New Delhi in 1980 and it would appear that another focus for Commonwealth activity has emerged, and one which may be imitated in other parts of the world.

It would be wrong to end this historical survey of the growth of the modern Commonwealth on a note of exaggerated optimism about a future which, in any case, the historian cannot foretell. By 1980, however, the Commonwealth has established itself as a uniquely effective international organisation, both as a forum for consultation and a medium of functional co-operation. To describe the Commonwealth in such prosaic terms is a far cry both from the frothy rhetoric of the Empire out of which it grew, and from sentimental and complacent post-war musings about the Commonwealth 'club' (a description which, incidentally, has always irritated Secretary-General Ramphal).

The *raison d'être* of the modern Commonwealth, however, lies in its essentially practical role: as a meeting place for 'North' and 'South'; as an agency which can provide technical and other assistance to a substantial proportion of the world's developing countries (including some of the smallest and poorest of them) – what Ramphal has called a 'programme for the small and weak'. In relation to Zimbabwe in 1979–80, the Commonwealth also showed that it could once again play a politically dynamic role by its contribution to the settlement and its implementation. Many member states have come to depend on the help and support which the Commonwealth can provide. Such a relationship is, of course, far healthier than the outmoded dependence of a colony on the imperial power. Nevertheless, for countries such as Tuvalu and the other small island states of the Pacific Commonwealth, the organisation performs a vital supportive function without the neo-colonial element necessarily present where the small state looks only to a larger neighbour or to the former imperial power.

There is, nevertheless, still room for sentiment and for talk of the 'spirit' of the Commonwealth. Although the 1971 Commonwealth Declaration spoke of a 'voluntary association of states', the Commonwealth has remained, as the British Prime Minister Stanley Baldwin described it at the opening of the last pre-war Imperial Conference in 1937, an 'association of peoples'. This is witnessed by the existence, alongside the official Commonwealth of ministerial meetings, technical assistance groups and the like, of a whole range of diverse activities and organisations of which perhaps the best known and certainly the most spectacular are the Commonwealth Games. As Ramphal said, fresh from the triumphs of the Lusaka Heads of Government Meeting: 'The Commonwealth is more than a conference, it is much more, – it is a way of life'.[24]

# APPENDIX

COMMONWEALTH MEMBERSHIP AS AT 31 DECEMBER
1980

|                     |   | Date of membership |                      |
|---------------------|---|--------------------|----------------------|
| Australia           | Q | (1901)             |                      |
| Bahamas             | Q | 1973               |                      |
| Bangladesh          | R | 1972               |                      |
| Barbados            | Q | 1966               |                      |
| Botswana            | R | 1966               |                      |
| Canada              | Q | (1867)             |                      |
| Cyprus              | R | 1961               | (independent 1960)   |
| Dominica            | R | 1978               |                      |
| Fiji                | Q | 1970               |                      |
| The Gambia          | R | 1965               |                      |
| Ghana               | R | 1957               |                      |
| Grenada             | Q | 1974               |                      |
| Guyana              | R | 1966               |                      |
| India               | R | 1947               |                      |
| Jamaica             | Q | 1962               |                      |
| Kenya               | R | 1963               |                      |
| Kiribati            | R | 1979               |                      |
| Lesotho             | M | 1966               |                      |
| Malawi              | R | 1964               |                      |
| Malaysia            | M | 1957               |                      |
| Malta               | R | 1964               |                      |
| Mauritius           | Q | 1968               |                      |
| Nauru*              | R | 1968               |                      |
| New Zealand         | Q | (1907)             |                      |
| Nigeria             | R | 1960               |                      |
| Papua New Guinea    | Q | 1975               |                      |

| | | | |
|---|---|---|---|
| St Lucia | Q | 1979 | |
| St Vincent* | Q | 1979 | |
| Seychelles | R | 1976 | |
| Sierra Leone | R | 1961 | |
| Singapore | R | 1965 | |
| Solomon Islands | Q | 1978 | |
| Sri Lanka | R | 1948 | |
| Swaziland | M | 1968 | |
| Tanzania | R | 1961 | |
| Tonga | M | 1970 | |
| Trinidad and Tobago | R | 1962 | |
| Tuvalu* | Q | 1979 | |
| Uganda | R | 1962 | |
| United Kingdom | Q | | |
| Vanuatu | R | 1980 | |
| Western Samoa | M | 1970 | (independent 1962) |
| Zambia | R | 1964 | |
| Zimbabwe | R | 1980 | |

*Key*
* Special member
Q Queen Elizabeth as Head of State
M Other monarchy
R Republic

*Note*: Belize and Antigua/Barbuda achieved independence in 1981, bringing the membership of the Commonwealth to forty-six. In each case Queen Elizabeth remained Head of State.

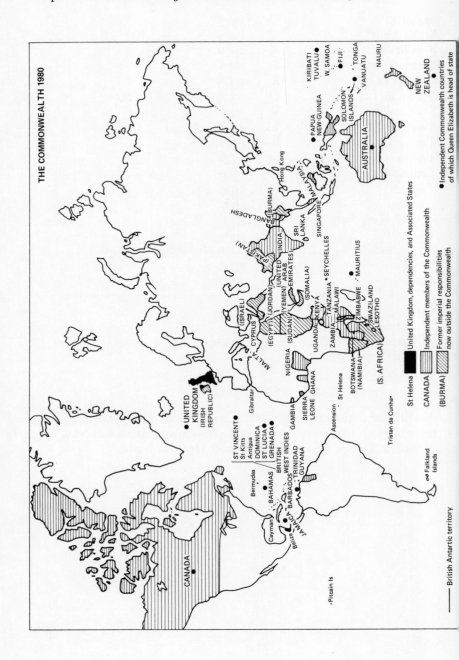

# NOTES

PART 1: THE EMPIRE AND IMPERIALISM IN 1902

1. British Library, Add. Mss. 49732, Curzon to Balfour, 31 March 1901.
2. See Denis Judd, *Radical Joe: a Life of Joseph Chamberlain* (1977); Peter Fraser, *Joseph Chamberlain* (1966); R. Jay, *Joseph Chamberlain* (1981).
3. See J. E. Flint, *Cecil Rhodes* (1976).
4. See David Dilks, *Curzon in India* (2 vols, 1969 and 1970).
5. See Terence O'Brien, *Milner* (1979) and A. M. Gollin, *Proconsul in Politics* (1964).
6. Austen Chamberlain papers, Birmingham University, Balfour to Austen Chamberlain, 31 December 1902.
7. See D. James, *Lord Roberts* (1954).
8. See Philip Magnus, *Kitchener: portrait of an Imperialist* (1958) and George H. Cassar, *Kitchener* (1977).
9. British Library Add. Mss. 49710, Fisher to Balfour, 19 October 1903.
10. *The Definitive Edition of Rudyard Kipling's Verse* (1949) p. 429.
11. Ibid., p. 328.
12. See Bernard Porter, *Critics of Empire* (1968), and A. P. Thornton, *The Imperial Idea and Its Enemies* (1959).
13. J. A. Hobson, *Imperialism: a study* (1902).

PART 2: CONSOLIDATION AND CATACLYSM, 1902-19

1. Denis Judd, *Balfour and the British Empire* (1968) pp. 306-11.
2. *Cambridge History of the British Empire*, vol. 3, (1959) pp. 431-6.
3. Denis Judd, *Balfour and the British Empire*, p. 305.
4. Ibid., and F. A. Johnson, *Defence by Committee* (1960).
5. Ibid.
6. Ibid.
7. See A. M. Gollin, *Balfour's Burden* (1965); Denis Judd, *Radical Joe* (1977); Peter Fraser, *Joseph Chamberlain* (1966); R. Jay, *Joseph Chamberlain* (1981).
8. Ibid.
9. Ibid.
10. Ibid.

11. See also Alan Sykes, *Tariff Reform in British Politics 1903–13* (1979) and J. Grigg, *Lloyd George*, vol. 2 (1978).
12. See J. E. Kendle, *The Colonial and Imperial Conferences 1887–1911* (1967).
13. Ibid.
14. *Selected Speeches and Documents on British Colonial Policy 1763–1917* (ed. A. B. Keith) (1961) p. 271.
15. See Walter Nimocks, *Milner's Young Men* (1970).
16. E. A. Walker, *A History of Southern Africa* (1957) p. 512.
17. See A. K. Russell, *Liberal Landslide: the General Election of 1906* (1973).
18. G. H. L. Le May, *British Supremacy in South Africa* (1965) pp. 198–202.
19. Judd, *Balfour and the British Empire*, p. 217; *Oxford History of South Africa*, vol. 2 (1971).
20. D. W. Kruger, *The Making of a Nation: the Union of South Africa 1910–1961* (1969).
21. See note 16 above.
22. See D. G. Creighton, *Dominion of the North* (2nd edn, 1958).
23. Ibid.
24. N. H. Carrier and J. R. Jeffery, *External Migration* (1953).
25. See J. A. La Nauze, *Alfred Deakin* (2 vols) (1965).
26. See *Cambridge History of the British Empire*, vol. 3 (1959) Ch. 12.
27. British Library Add. Mss. 49732, Curzon to Balfour, 31 March 1901.
28. Ibid.
29. See PRO Cab. 37/19/154 for Balfour's analysis of the dangers of Curzon's 'independent' foreign policy.
30. S. A. Wolpert, *Morley and India 1906–10* (1967) p. 231.
31. See S. R. Mehrotra, *India and the Commonwealth* (1965) pp. 43–5.
32. Ibid., and R. J. Moore, *Liberalism and Indian Politics 1872–1922* (1966); S. Koss, *John Morley at the India Office* (1969).
33. S. R. Wasti, *Lord Minto and the Indian Nationalist Movement 1905–10* (1964).
34. See L. H. Gann and Peter Duignan (eds.), *African Proconsuls* (1978) pp. 209–353.
35. *Cambridge History of the British Empire*, vol. 3, p. 605.
36. Ibid., pp. 641–2.
37. Ibid., p. 642.
38. Quoted in Lord Ronaldshay, *Life of Lord Curzon*, vol. 3, (1928) p. 168.
39. See Mehrotra, op. cit.
40. See A. B. Keith op. cit., pp. 376–403.
41. See *Cambridge History of the British Empire*, vol. 3, ch. 17.

PART 3: THE EMPIRE/COMMONWEALTH AT PEACE, 1919–39

1. B. Porter, *The Lion's Share: a Short History of British Imperialism 1850–1970* (1975), p. 258.
2. P. Mansfield, *The British in Egypt* (1971) p. 242.
3. R. G. Gregory, *India and East Africa: a History of Race Relations within the British Empire 1890–1939* (1971) p. 197.
4. Memorandum relating to Indians in Kenya, Cmd 1922 (1923) p. 10.

5. E. Huxley, *White Man's Country: Lord Delamere and the Making of Kenya* (1935) vol. 2, p. 155.

6. L. H. Gann, *A History of Northern Rhodesia* (1964) pp. 240–1.

7. Joint Select Committee: Report HC 156 (1931) p. 31.

8. *Rhodesia and Nyasaland Royal Commission Report*, Cmd 5949 (1939).

9. Quoted in H. F. Morris and J. S. Read, *Indirect Rule and the Search for Justice* (1972) p. 3.

10. A. G. Hopkins, *An Economic History of West Africa* (1973) p. 190.

11. L. S. Amery, *National and Imperial Economics* (1923) p. 70.

12. *West Indies Royal Commission Report*, Cmd 6607 (1945). Publication was delayed until after the war.

13. L. R. James, *Beyond the Boundary* (1963) pp. 120–2.

14. *Ceylon: Report of the Special Commission on the Constitution*, Cmd 3131 (1928) (Donoughmore Report).

15. Lord Butler, *The Art of the Possible* (1971) p. 41. Butler was Parliamentary Under-Secretary of State for India, 1932–7.

16. Ibid., p. 16.

17. A. B. Keith (ed), *Speeches and Documents on the British Dominions 1918–1931* (1932) pp. 62–5.

18. Irwin's own ambivalent attitude to the meaning of dominion status in the Indian context (he admitted to Lord Salisbury shortly before the declaration was issued in October 1929 that the 'realisation of the aspiration is not in sight') is revealed by G. Peele, 'A Note on the Irwin Declaration', *Journal of Imperial and Commonwealth History*, 1 (1972–3) 331.

19. Quoted in R. Rhodes James, *Churchill: A Study in Failure* (1970) p. 202.

20. Quoted in D. A. Low, *Lion Rampant: Essays in the Study of British Imperialism* (1973) p. 161.

21. Quoted in H. Macmillan, *The Winds of Change, 1914–1939* (1966) p. 318.

22. Butler, op. cit., p. 54.

23. Quoted in R. Rhodes James, op. cit., p. 202.

24. Low, op. cit., pp. 170, 172.

25. H. Duncan Hall, *Commonwealth: A History of the British Commonwealth of Nations* (1971) p. 393.

26. Keith, op. cit., p. 161. This formula is sometimes referred to as the 'Balfour Declaration', but it should not be confused with the 'Balfour Declaration' of 1917 relating to the establishment of a national home for the Jews in Palestine.

27. Hall, op. cit., p. 637.

28. House of Commons, 20 November 1931, quoted in Keith, op. cit., p. 274.

29. Hall, op. cit., p. 365.

30. Keith, op. cit., p. 318.

31. J. B. D. Miller, *Britain and the Old Dominions* (1966) pp. 119–20.

32. The Kingston Communiqué, 1975, para. 27 *et seq.* Below, p. 139.

33. David Carlton, 'The Dominions and British Policy in the Abyssinian Crisis', *Journal of Imperial and Commonwealth History*, 1 (1972–3) 59.

34. K. Middlemas, *The Diplomacy of Illusion* (1972) pp. 21–3.

35. Quoted in Hall, op. cit., p. 755.

36. Quoted in M. Perham, *Colonial Sequence, 1930–1949* (1967) p. 124.

37. D. W. Harkness, *The Restless Dominion: the Irish Free State and the British Commonwealth of Nations* (1969) p. 13; Hall, op. cit., p. 811.

PART 4: THE SECOND WORLD WAR AND ITS AFTERMATH, 1939–51

1. See C. Cross, *The Fall of the British Empire* (1968); J. Morris, *Farewell the Trumpets* (1978); B. Porter, *The Lion's Share* (1975); N. Mansergh, *The Commonwealth Experience* (1969).
2. W. K. Hancock, *Smuts*, vol. 2 (1968) and R. W. Kruger, *The Making of a Nation: the Union of South Africa 1910–1961* (1969).
3. D. W. Harkness, *The Restless Dominion* (1969).
4. See H. V. Hodson, *The Great Divide* (1969).
5. See J. M. Lee, *Colonial Development and Good Government* (1967).
6. See E. Monroe, *Britain's Moment in the Middle East* (1963) pp. 89–94.
7. See W. S. Churchill, *The Second World War*, vol. 3, (1950); vol. 4 (1951).
8. See R. J. Moore, *Churchill, Cripps and India 1939–45* (1979).
9. See E. W. R. Lumby, and N. Mansergh, (eds) *Constitutional Relations Between Britain and India. The Transfer of Power 1942–7*, vol. 2, 'Quit India' (1971).
10. See R. L. Louis, *Imperialism at Bay* (1978).
11. See P. S. Gupta, *Imperialism and the British Labour Movement* (1975).
12. See B. N. Pandey, *The Break up of British India* (1969); E. W. R. Lumby, *The Transfer of Power in India* (1954); C. H. Philips and M. D. Wainwright, *The Partition of India* (1970).
13. A. Campbell-Johnson, *Mission with Mountbatten* (1951) and R. Hough, *Mountbatten: Hero of Our Time* (1980).
14. Lumby and Mansergh op. cit.
15. K. K. Aziz, *The Making of Pakistan* (1967); Penderel Moon, *Divide and Quit* (1961); Lumby and Mansergh, op. cit.
16. Declaration of London, Final Communiqué of the Prime Minister's Meeting, 1949.
17. P. Gordon Walker, *The Commonwealth* (1962) p. 315.
18. P. S. Gupta, *Imperialism and the British Labour Movement* (1975) p. 305.
19. B. Porter, op. cit. p. 318.
20. Colonial Office paper No. 206, 1946. See generally, D. J. Morgan, *The Official History of Colonial Development*, vol. 5, *Guidance towards Self-Government in British Colonies 1941–1971* (1980); J. M. Lee, *Colonial Development and Good Government* (1967).
21. Seretse Khama, heir to the Chieftaincy of the Bamangwato tribe in Bechuanaland, was exiled in 1950. He had married an Englishwoman, Ruth Williams, and his enforced exile was seen by many on the left in Britain as a race issue. He was subsequently restored, and died in 1980.
22. D. Goldsworthy, *Colonial Issues in British Politics 1945–1961* (1971) p. 142; G. Bennett, *Kenya: A Political History* (1963) pp. 106–7.
23. D. Austin, *Politics in Ghana 1946–1960* (1964).


PART 5: THE COMMONWEALTH IN TRANSITION, 1951–65

1. H. Macmillan, *Pointing the Way, 1959–1961* (1972) pp. 116–17.
2. *The Memoirs of Lord Chandos* (1962) p. 355.
3. *Hansard*, House of Commons Debates, fifth series, vol. 531, col. 509.
4. C. Cross, *The Fall of the British Empire* (1968) p. 310. For a first-hand account of

the Cyprus crisis, see Sir Hugh Foot (later Lord Caradon), *A Start in Freedom* (1964) ch. 9.

5. Chandos, op. cit., p. 394.
6. G. Bennett, *Kenya: A Political History* (1963) p. 135.
7. *Report of the Nyasaland Commission of Inquiry*, Cmnd 814 (1959) p. 1.
8. H. Macmillan, *At the End of the Day* (1973) p. 311.
9. *Report of the Advisory Commission on Review of the Federal Constitution* (Mockton Report) Cmnd 1148 (1960).
10. D. J. Morgan, *The Official History of Colonial Development*, vol. 5 (1980) pp. 93, 251 *et seq*.
11. D. Goldsworthy, *Colonial Issues in British Politics 1945–1961* (1971) p. 361.
12. Macmillan (1973) op. cit.
13. See below, p. 000.
14. Macmillan (1973) op. cit., p. 312.
15. L. S. Amery, *My Political Life*, vol. 1 (1953) p. 16.
16. B. Porter, *The Lion's Share* (1975) p. 336.
17. Quoted in J. B. Watson, *Empire to Commonwealth* (1971) p. 247.
18. Macmillan (1973) op. cit., pp. 1–34.
19. See Hugh Thomas, *The Suez Affair* (1967); Harold Macmillan, *Riding the Storm* (1971); Anthony Nutting, *No End of a Lesson* (1967).

PART 6: CRISIS IN CONFIDENCE, 1966–71

1. See George Hutchinson, *Edward Heath* (1970) chs 8 and 9, and Appendix I, 'Realism in British Foreign Policy', by Edward Heath.
2. See Harold Wilson, *The Labour Government 1964–70* (1971) pp. 108–13, 625–6.
3. Ibid., pp. 311–14, 567–70, 575–7.
4. Quoted in J. B. Watson, *Empire to Commonwealth* (1971) p. 238.
5. For Nkrumah's version of events see his *Dark Days in Ghana* (1968).
6. John de St Jorre, *The Nigerian Civil War* (1972).
7. See Tom Mboya, *Freedom and After* (1963) and A. Marshall Macphee, *Kenya* (1968).
8. See Richard Hall, *Zambia* (1965).
9. See Lord Brockway, *The Colonial Revolution* (1973).
10. J. B. Watson, op. cit., p. 256.
11. See J. Kennedy, *A History of Malaya* (2nd edn 1970), and D. G. E. Hall, *A History of South-East Asia* (3rd edn 1968).

PART 7: THE COMMONWEALTH REVIVED, 1971–80

1. N. Mansergh, *The Commonwealth Experience* (1969) pp. 410–11.
2. Lord Garner, *The Commonwealth Office, 1925–68* (1978) p. 439. Siéyès was speaking of his experiences during the French Revolution.
3. *Commonwealth Heads of Government: The London Communiqué, 1977* paragraph 35 (Commonwealth Secretariat).
4. For a useful summary of the provisions of this constitution, see Read, *Commonwealth Law Bulletin*, 6 (1980) 262.

5. Ibid., 278.
6. The GNP per capita was estimated in 1977 as $90 for Bangladesh, $200 for mainland Tanzania (*World Bank Atlas*, 1978). In other words the average Bangladeshi can expect to receive each year a notional £50 share of the national income.
7. *The Report of the Royal Commission on the Constitution* (Kilbrandon Report) Cmnd 5460 (1973) contains a wealth of material; on devolution, see V. Bogdanor, *Devolution* (1979).
8. See above, p. 63.
9. Byng refused Liberal Prime Minister Mackenzie King a dissolution and then granted one to his Conservative successor; the latter lost the ensuing general election.
10. Above, p. 111.
11. Address to the *Sixth Commonwealth Law Conference, Lagos, Nigeria*, 22 August 1980.
12. West Indian federation was destroyed by island separatism.
13. *Report on the Supply of Petroleum . . . to Rhodesia* by T. H. Bingham, QC and S. M. Gray, FCA (1978) (the 'Bingham Report').
14. For a summary, see P. Slinn, *Commonwealth Law Bulletin*, 6 (1980), 1045.
15. For the record of this historic conference, see *Southern Rhodesia: Report of the Constitutional Conference*, Cmnd 7802 (1980).
16. *Final Report of the Commonwealth Observer Group on the Southern Rhodesia Elections, February 1980*, Commonwealth Secretariat (1980). This unique record repays careful study.
17. The island of Hong Kong and the mainland on which Kowloon now stands were ceded outright by China in 1842 and 1860 respectively. The 'New Territories', the rural hinterland of Kowloon, were leased for 99 years in 1898. China subsequently denounced all such 'unequal treaties' and appears to regard the British presence on 'Chinese' territory as being on sufferance.
18. Compare figures given in *Commonwealth Relations Office Year Book* (1966) and *Year Book of the Commonwealth* (1979).
19. *Final Communiqué, Commonwealth Heads of Government Meeting Lusaka, August 1979*, paragraph 48 (Commonwealth Secretariat).
20. *The Report of the Independent Commission on International Development Issues under the Chairmanship of Willy Brandt* (1980).
21. *Commonwealth Skills for Commonwealth Needs: Commonwealth Fund for Technical Co-operation*, Commonwealth Secretariat (1981).
22. *Seventh Report to the Heads of Government by the Commonwealth Secretary General* (1979).
23. This declaration became known as the 'Gleneagles Agreement' from the venue of the Heads of Government weekend retreat at the 1977 Conference. The agreement averted a threatened boycott of the Commonwealth Games due to take place in Edmonton, Canada, in 1978.
24. Address to the Royal Institute of International Affairs, London, 21 September 1979.

# SELECT BIBLIOGRAPHY

The bibliography consists of books that the authors have found useful and that provide appropriate further reading. Where a book has been mentioned in the notes it has not necessarily been included in the bibliography.

## GENERAL BOOKS

Beloff, M., *Imperial Sunset*, vol. 1, *1897–1921* (1969).
Barnett, Correlli, *The Collapse of British Power* (1972).
Bowle, John, *The Imperial Achievement* (1974).
Brockway, Fenner, *The Colonial Revolution* (1973).
*Cambridge History of the British Empire*, vol. 3 (1959).
Cross, Colin, *The Fall of the British Empire* (1968).
Cumpston, I. M. (ed.) *The Growth of the British Commonwealth, 1880–1932* (1973).
Faber, R., *The Vision and the Need* (1966).
Fieldhouse, D. K., *The Colonial Empire* (1966).
—— *Colonialism, 1870–1945* (1981).
Grierson, Edward, *The Imperial Dream* (1972).
Grimal, Henri, *Decolonization* (English translation 1978).
Gordon, Walker, P., *The Commonwealth* (1962).
Hall, Duncan, H., *Commonwealth: a History of the British Commonwealth* (1971).
Kiernan, V. G., *Marxism and Imperialism* (1974).
Koebner, R. and Schmidt, H. D., *Imperialism: 1840–1960* (1964).
Low, D. A., *Lion Rampant* (1973).
Mansergh, N., *The Commonwealth Experience* (1969; 2nd edition in 2 vols 1982).
Morris, J., *Farewell the Trumpets* (vol. 3 of *Pax Britannica* trilogy) (1978).
MacIntyre, W. D., *Colonies into Commonwealth* (1966).
——*The Commonwealth of Nations* (1977).
Macmillan, W. M., *The Road to Self-Rule* (1959).
Porter, Bernard, *The Lion's Share* (1970).
Perham, M., *The Colonial Reckoning* (1963).
Thornton, A. P., *The Imperial Idea and Its Enemies* (1959).
Watson, J. B., *Empire to Commonwealth* (1971).
Woodcock, George, *Who Killed the British Empire?* (1974).

# THE OLD COMMONWEALTH

## General Books

Dawson, R. M., *The Development of Dominion Status* (1937).

Doxey, M., 'Continuity and Change in the Commonwealth', *Year Book of World Affairs*, vol. 33 (1979).

Evatt, H. V., *The King and his Dominion Governors* (1967).

Garner, J., *The Commonwealth Office* (1978).

Gordon, D. C., *The Dominion Partnership in Imperial Defence* (1965).

Hancock, W. K., *Survey of British Commonwealth Affairs* (1942).

Judd, D., *Balfour and the British Empire* (1968).

Kendle, J. E., *The Colonial and Imperial Conferences 1887–1911* (1967).

Miller, J. D. B., *Britain and the Old Dominions* (1966).

—— *Survey of British Commonwealth Affairs: problems of expansion and attrition 1953–1969* (1974).

Morgan, D. J., *The Official History of Colonial Development*, especially vol. 5, *Guidance Towards Self-government in British Colonies* (1980).

Wheare, K. C., *The Statute of Westminster and Dominion Status* (5th edn 1953).

## Some Memoirs of 'Commonwealth Men'

Butler, Lord, *The Art of the Possible* (1971).

Chandos, Viscount, *The Memoirs of Lord Chandos* (1962).

Foot, Sir Hugh, *A Start in Freedom* (1964).

Kaunda, K., *Zambia shall be Free: an Autobiography* (1963).

Macmillan, H., *Memoirs*, vols I–VI (1966–73).

Nkrumah, K., *Ghana* (1957).

Smith, Arnold, *Stitches in Time; the Commonwealth in World Politics* (1981).

Welensky, Sir Roy, *Welensky's 4000 Days* (1964).

## Australia

Alexander, F., *Australia since Federation* (1967).

Barnard, Marjorie, *A History of Australia* (1962).

Clark, C. M. H., *A Short History of Australia* (1963).

Crowley, Frank (ed), *A New History of Australia* (1974).

—— *Modern Australia in Documents* (1973).

La Nauze, J. A., *Alfred Deakin* (1965).

Menzies, R. G., *Afternoon Light* (1967).

—— *The Measure of the Years* (1970).

Miller, J. D. B., *Australian Government and Politics* (4th edn 1971).

Preston, R. (ed), *Contemporary Australia: Studies in History, Politics and Economics* (1969).

Reese, Trevor R., *Australia in the Twentieth Century* (1964).

Shaw, A. G. L., *The Story of Australia* (2nd edn 1961).

Younger, R. M., *Australia and the Australians* (1970).

## Canada

Creighton, D., *Dominion of the North* (1958).
—— *Canada's First Century, 1867–1967* (1970).
Dawson, R. M., *William Lyon Mackenzie King* (1958).
Graham, G. S., *Canada* (1950).
McGregor, F. A., *The Fall and Rise of Mackenzie King* (1962).
McNaught, K., *The Pelican History of Canada* (revised edn 1976).
Morton, W. L., *The Canadian Identity* (2nd edn 1972).
Pearson, Lester, *Memoirs*, vol. 1 1897–1948 (1973); vol. 2, 1948–1957 (1974).
Reid, J. H. Stewart *et al.* (eds), *A Source Book of Canadian History* (1959).
Schull, J., *Laurier* (1965).
Trudeau, Pierre E., *Federalism and the French Canadians* (1968).
Wade, M. *The French Canadians*, vol. 1 (1968); vol. 2 (1968).

## New Zealand

Burdon, R. M., *The New Dominion* (1965).
Condliffe, J. B., *New Zealand in the Making* (2nd edn 1959).
Firth, R., *Economics of the New Zealand Maori* (1959).
Miller, H., *New Zealand* (1950).
Oliver, W. H., *The Story of New Zealand* (1960).
Reeves, W. P., *The Long White Cloud* (1923).
Rowe, J. W. and Margaret A., *New Zealand* (1967).
Sinclair, K., *A History of New Zealand* (1959).

## South Africa

Adams, H., *Modernising Racial Domination* (1971).
Ballinger, M., *From Union to Apartheid* (1964).
Davenport, T. R. H., *South Africa: a Modern History* (2nd edn 1978).
Hancock, K., *Smuts*, vol. 1 (1965); vol. 2 (1968).
Heever, van den C. M., *General J. B. M. Hertzog* (1946).
Hyam, R., *The Failure of South African Expansion, 1908–48* (1972).
Kruger, D. W., *The Making of a Nation* (1969).
Le May, G. H. L., *British Supremacy in South Africa 1899–1907* (1965).
Mansergh, N., *South Africa, 1906–61: the Price of Magnanimity* (1962).
Meintjes, J., *General Louis Botha* (1970).
*Oxford History of South Africa* (eds Wilson and Thompson), vol. 2 (1971).
Robertson, J., *Liberalism in South Africa* (1971).
Scholtz, G. D., *Dr H. F. Verwoerd* (1974).
Thompson, L. M., *The Unification of South Africa, 1902–10* (1960).
Troup, Freda, *South Africa: an Historical Introduction* (1972).
Walker, E. A., *A History of Southern Africa* (new impression, with corrections, 1968).

# INDIA AND PAKISTAN

Allen, C., (ed), *Plain Tales from the Raj* (1975).
Ali, C. M., *The Emergence of Pakistan* (1967).
Ashe, G., *Gandhi: A Study in Revolution* (1968).
Aziz, K. K., *Britain and Muslim India* (1963).
Blackburn, R. (ed), *Explosion in a Sub-continent* (1975).
Bolitho, H., *Jinnah* (1954).
Brown, Judith, *Gandhi's Rise to Power, 1915–22* (1972).
—— *Gandhi and Civil Disobedience, 1928–34* (1976).
Campbell-Johnson, A., *Mission with Mountbatten* (1951).
Edwardes, M., *British India* (1967).
Gandhi, M. K., *An Autobiography, or the Story of my Experiments with Truth* (1966).
Gopal, S., *The Viceroyalty of Lord Irwin* (1957).
Hamid, A., *Muslim Separatism in India* (1967).
Hodson, H. V., *The Great Divide* (1969).
Low, D. A. (ed), *Congress and the Raj* (1978).
Mehrotra, S. R., *India and the Commonwealth* (1965).
Mehta, V., *Mahatma Gandhi and his Apostles* (1977).
Moore, R. J., *Crisis of Indian Unity* (1974).
Mosley, L., *The Last Days of the British Raj* (1962).
Nanda, B. R., *Mahatma Gandhi* (1958).
—— *Gokhale, Gandhi and the Nehrus* (1974).
—— *Gandhi and Nehru* (1980).
Nehru, J., *An Autobiography* (1942).
Pandey, B. N., *The Break-up of British India* (1969).
—— *Nehru* (1976).
Robb, P. G., *The Government of India and Reform* (1976).
Selbourne, D., *An Eye to India* [the Emergency of 1975] (1977).
Smith, W. R., *Nationalism and Reform in India* (1966).
Spear, P., *The Oxford History of Modern India* (2nd edn 1978).
Symonds, R. A., *The Making of Pakistan* (1950).

# THE AFRICAN COMMONWEALTH

Allen, C. (ed), *Tales from the Dark Continent* (1979).
Austin, D., *Politics in Africa* (1978).
Gann, L. H. and Duignan, P. (eds), *Colonialism in Africa*, vol. II (1969); vol. III (1971).
Oliver, R. and Atmore, A., *Africa since 1800* (1981).
Rotberg, R. I. and Mazrui, A., *Protest and Power in Black Africa* (1970).

## *East Africa*

Bennett, G., *Kenya: A Political History* (1963).
Gregory, R. G., *India and East Africa: a History of Race Relations within the British Empire 1890–1939* (1971).

Harlow, V. and Chilver, E. M. (eds), *History of East Africa*, vol. II (1965).
Iliffe, J., *A Modern History of Tanganiyka* (1979).
Karugire, S. R., *A Political History of Uganda* (1980).

## Central Africa

Blake, R., *A History of Rhodesia* (1977).
Martin, D. and Johnson, P., *The Struggle for Zimbabwe* (1981).
Roberts, A., *A History of Zambia* (1976).
Rotberg, R. I., *The Rise of Nationalism in Central Africa: the making of Malawi and Zambia 1873–1964* (1966).
Wills, A. J., *An Introduction to the History of Central Africa* (3rd edn 1973).

## West Africa

Austin, D., *Politics in Ghana 1946–1960* (1964).
Burns, A., *History of Nigeria* (1978).
Crowder, M., *West Africa under Colonial Rule* (1968).
—— *The Story of Nigeria* (4th edn 1978).
Davidson, B., *Black Star* [Nkrumah] (1973).
Fage, J. D., *An Introduction to the History of West Africa* (1962).
Ward, W. E. F., *A History of Ghana* (1958).

# CEYLON AND THE WEST INDIES

## Sri Lanka

Ludowyk, E. F. C., *The Modern History of Ceylon* (1966).
'Zeylanicus', *Ceylon* (1970).

## West Indies

Burns, A., *A History of the British West Indies* (1954).
Lewis, G. K., *The Growth of the Modern West Indies* (1968).
Sherlock, P., *West Indian Nations: a New History* (1973).
Williams, E., *From Columbus to Castro: the History of the Caribbean 1492–1969* (1970).

# INDEX